Workbook 8

Project Management

Manage Resources
Certificate
S/NVQ Level 4

Institute of Management Open Learning Programme

Series editor: Gareth Lewis
Author: Cathy Lake

*the Institute
of Management*

F O U N D A T I O N

**Pergamon
Open
Learning**

Pergamon Open Learning
An imprint of Butterworth-Heinemann
Linacre House, Jordan Hill, Oxford OX2 8DP
225 Wildwood Avenue, Woburn, MA 01801-2041
A division of Reed Educational and Professional Publishing Ltd

℞ A member of the Reed Elsevier plc group

OXFORD   BOSTON   JOHANNESBURG
MELBOURNE   NEW DELHI   SINGAPORE

First published 1997
Reprinted 1998

British Library Cataloguing in Publication Data
A catalogue record for this book is available from the British Library

ISBN 0 7506 3667 X

Typeset by Avocet Typeset, Brill, Aylesbury, Bucks
Printed and bound in Great Britain

PLANT A TREE
BTCV
British Trust for
Conservation Volunteers

FOR EVERY TITLE THAT WE PUBLISH, BUTTERWORTH-HEINEMANN
WILL PAY FOR BTCV TO PLANT AND CARE FOR A TREE.

Contents

Series overview

The Institute of Management Open Learning Programme is a series of workbooks prepared by the Institute of Management and Pergamon Open Learning for managers seeking to develop themselves.

Comprising seventeen open learning workbooks, the programme covers the best of modern management theory and practice, and each workbook provides a range of frameworks and techniques to improve your effectiveness as a manager, thus helping you acquire the knowledge and skill to make you fully competent in your role.

Each workbook is written by an experienced management writer and covers an important management topic or theme. The activities both reinforce learning and help to relate the generic ideas to your individual work context. While coverage of each topic is fully comprehensive, additional reading suggestions and reference sources are given for those who wish to study to a greater depth.

Designed to be practical, stimulating and challenging, the aim of the workbooks is to improve performance at work by benefiting you and your organization. This practical focus is at the heart of the competence based approach that has been adopted by the programme.

The structure of the programme

The design and overall structure of the programme has two main organizing principles, both of which are closely linked to the national standards for management developed by the MCI (Management Charter Initiative).

First, the workbooks are grouped according to the key roles of management.

- Underpinning the management standards are a series of **personal competences** which describe the personal skills required by all managers, which are essential to skill in all the main functional or key role areas.
- **Manage Activities** describes the principles of managing processes and activities, with service to the customer as an essential part of this.
- **Manage Resources** describes the acquisition, control and monitoring of financial and other resources.
- **Manage People** looks at the key skills involved in leadership, developing one's staff and managing their performance.

■ **Manage Information** discusses the acquisition, storage and use of information for communication, problem solving and decision making.

In addition, there are three specialized key roles: **Manage Quality, Manage Projects** and **Manage Energy**. The workbooks cover the first two of these. Unlike the four primary key roles above, these are not compulsory for certificate, diploma or S/NVQ requirements, but provide options for the latter.

Together, these key roles provide a comprehensive description of the fundamental principles of management as it applies in any organization – commercial, maintained sector or not-for-profit.

Second, the programme is organized according to **levels of management**, seniority and responsibility.

Level 4 represents first line management. In accredited programmes this is equivalent to S/NVQ Level 4, Certificate in Management or CMS. Level 5 is equivalent to middle/senior management and is accredited at S/NVQ Level 5, Diploma in Management or DMS. There are two S/NVQs at Level 5: Operational Management and Strategic Management. The operations role is focussed internally within an organization on the maintenance of systems and standards of output, whilst the strategic role is focussed on the whole organization, including the external operating environment, and looks at setting directions.

Together, the workbooks cover all the background knowledge you need to have for all units of competence in the MCI standards at Level 4 and Level 5 (apart from the specialized units in the key role Manage Energy). They also provide skills development and opportunities for portfolio building.

For a comprehensive list of workbooks, see page ix. For a comprehensive list of links with the standards, see the *User Guide.*

How to use the programme

The programme is deliberately designed to be flexible and can be used in a variety of ways:

■ to update on important management topics and themes, or develop individual skills: as the workbooks are grouped according to themes, it should be easy for you to pick out one that suits your needs

■ as part of generic management development programmes: you can choose the modules that fit the themes of the programme

■   as part of, and in support of, accredited competence-based programmes.

For N/SVQs at both Levels 4 and 5, there are options in the combinations of units that make up the various awards. By using the map provided in the *User Guide*, individuals will be able to select the workbooks appropriate to their specific needs, and their chosen accreditation options. Some of the activities will help you provide evidence for your portfolio; where we think this is the case, we give the relevant reference to the standards.

For Certificate or CMS, Diploma or DMS, individuals should choose modules that not only meet their individual needs but also satisfy the requirements of the delivering body and the awarding body.

You may need help and guidance in these choices, and the *User Guide* sets out the options and advice in much more detail. A fuller description of the potential uses of this material in evidence gathering and portfolio building can also be found in the *User Guide*, as can a detailed description of the contents of each workbook.

Workbooks in the Institute of Management Open Learning Programme

Manage People (Level 5)

14 *The New Model Leader*

Manage Information (Level 4)

15 *Making Rational Decisions*
16 *Communication*

Manage Information (Level 5)

17 *Successful Information Management*

Manage Quality (Level 4)

3 *Understanding Business Process Management**
4 *Customer Focus**

Manage Quality (Level 5)

5 *Getting TQM to Work**

Manage Projects (Level 4)

8 *Project Management**

Manage Projects (Level 5)

8 *Project Management**

Support Materials

18 *User Guide*
19 *Mentor Guide*

An asterisk indicates that a particular workbook also contains material suitable for a particular key role or personal competence over and above that where it is principally designated.

Links to qualifications

S/NVQ programmes

This workbook can help candidates to achieve credit and develop skills in the key role of managing resources at level 4, and covers the following units and elements:

B2   Manage the use of physical resources
B2.1   Plan the use of physical resources
B2.2   Obtain physical resources
B2.3   Ensure availability of supplies
B2.4   Monitor the use of physical resources

Likewise, it will also help candidates to achieve credit and develop skills in the key role Manage Projects and covers the following units and elements:

G1   Contribute to project planning and preparation
Gl. 1   Clarify the project's scope and definition
G1.2   Provide plans to achieve the project's goals
G1.3   Contribute to project preparation
G2   Co-ordinate the running of projects
G2.1   Support the project team
G2.   Co-ordinate activities, resources and plans
G2.3   Keep stakeholders informed of project progress
G3   Contribute to project closure
G3.1   Complete project activities
G3.2   Contribute to the evaluation of project planning and implementation
G4   Plan and prepare projects
G4.1   Agree the project's scope and definition with the sponsor
G4.2   Develop plans to achieve the project's goals
G4.3   Establish the project's resourcing and control methods
G5   Manage the running of projects
G5.1   Lead the project team
G5.2   Monitor and adjust activities, resources and plans
G5.3   Develop solutions to project problems
G5.4   Maintain communication with project stakeholders
G6   Complete project links
G6.1   Ensure the completion of project activities
G6.2   Evaluate the effectiveness of project planning and implementation

Certificate and Diploma programmes

This workbook, together with the other level 4 workbook on managing resources (9 – *Budgeting and Financial Control*), covers all of the knowledge required in the key role managing resources for Certificate in Management and CMS programmes.

Links to other workbooks

Other workbooks in the key role Manage Resources at Level 4 are:

9 *Budgeting and Financial Control*

and at Level 5:

10 *Effective Financial and Resource Management*

The theme of this workbook is closely associated with:

15 *Making Rational Decisions*

Introduction

A project starts with an idea. Somebody, somewhere in the organization, gets an idea about something which is not happening at the moment, but looks as though it might be worth doing. It could be a small idea:

> 'Perhaps we could set up some kind of car-share scheme and get more people into work when there's a tube strike.'

or it could be a very big idea indeed:

> 'If we invest in the development of this new vegetable protein now, we could be world leaders in three years time.'

Some projects never get further than the ideas stage. However, assuming a project **does** get off the ground, there will shortly come a point when one individual, the project manager, is given the task of turning the idea into a reality. In order to do this, he or she will need resources. These can take a variety of forms. For example, all the car-share scheme might require are:

- an eye-catching poster for the staff noticeboard
- some guidance from an insurance company
- a couple of hours' time to match lifts and passengers
- a word-processor and printer to write memos to all the participants

For the development of a totally new product, requirements might include:

- a major financial investment from shareholders
- a team of food scientists with specialized skills and a trained workforce to support them
- a market research report
- a new factory equipped with machinery

Whatever the scale of the project, it is the project manager who is largely responsible for identifying the necessary resources and making sure that they are used effectively. This workbook describes the skills and techniques necessary to do this successfully and competently.

Objectives

By the end of this workbook you should be able to:

■ understand the organizational context of resource planning, and how internal and external factors influence the use of resources

■ organize team roles and responsibilities

■ plan the effective use of resources

■ apply techniques to secure and use resources

■ understand the key factors in defining a project

■ plan, manage and deliver a project using appropriate tools and techniques

Section 1 Resources for projects

What is a project?

In 1961 President J F Kennedy set the United States an extraordinary target:

'... to land a man on the moon ... before the decade is over.'

Over the next few years the expertise and energy of hundreds of scientists and engineers were harnessed, new technologies were developed and billions of dollars were spent to achieve this aim. In 1969 Neil Armstrong stepped on the moon – and President Kennedy's target had been met five months ahead of schedule.

The Apollo Project has been described as the greatest human achievement of all time. It caught the public imagination in many different ways. For managers it demonstrated the astonishing results that can be produced when the tools and techniques of project management are used to focus resources on a particular goal. Since the 1960s, projects have become a part of life in all types of organizations. Projects are set up when businesses want to take 'a giant leap' into the future, and also in much more ordinary situations in which a definite outcome is required within a limited time.

You have probably already participated in several projects yourself.

ACTIVITY 1

Imagine that your manager asks to you to come and have a few words in his or her office. Your manager says 'I've got a project here which I think may interest you' ... and slides a folder across the desk towards you.

Before you open the folder, what is your instant, unspoken reaction? Note it down here.

How will I get time to do it!

FEEDBACK

Typical reactions in this situation might include:

- 'This sounds exciting!'
- 'This could be a break from routine.'
- 'Oh good, a chance to show what I'm capable of.'
- 'On top of everything else I've got on my plate at the moment? You must be joking.'

Whether your first reaction is positive or negative will probably depend on your previous experience of working on projects in your organization. You will, however, have realized that you are being given responsibility for something which is outside your normal workload. Projects are non-routine. They also have certain other characteristics.

Specific outcomes

Projects can be set up to achieve many different things, but in every case, after a project has finished, something exists which was wasn't there when it started. Sometimes the outcome of a project has a physical form, such as a completed building, a new product or a printed report. A project can also have a less tangible outcome, such as raised public awareness of a particular issue.

Instruments of change

Projects are a way of bringing about change. They are used to develop new products and systems or to alter the physical or intellectual environment. The word 'project' is actually derived from the Latin verb *proicere*, which means 'to throw forward'. A project is a leap into the future.

Sequence of tasks

A project always involves a sequence of activities which demand different resources and skills. The construction of a building, for example, uses the skills of surveyors, architects, bricklayers, plumbers, carpenters, electricians, and painters and decorators at various stages of the process.

Resource use

In a project, resources are brought together to achieve a particular aim. This combination of resources is unique to the project. In a project of any size, these resources invariably include people with a variety of different skills. They may also include information, time, equipment, materials, services, finance and energy. We will look at resources again later in this section.

Limited timespan

Every project has a definite beginning and end. Depending on the scale of the project, these points may be only a few hours or days apart, or be separated by several years. The outcomes which a project was designed to produce usually outlast the project itself.

Responsibility

Projects need firm direction and leadership. For this reason the responsibility for a project is usually given to a single individual or agency, who usually make a personal and professional commitment to its successful completion. A small project may be given to someone in addition to their everyday work. A large project will require the appointment of a dedicated project manager.

We can now put these characteristics together to form the following definition of a project:

> A project is a connected sequence of activities involving a range of resources, designed to achieve a particular outcome and frequently used as an instrument of change. It takes place within a defined period of time and is the responsibility of a single individual or agency.

ACTIVITY 2

Think of something in which you have been involved in the past which you think could probably be described as a project.

Answer these questions about it:

1 What outcome was it designed to achieve?

    To reduce rent arrears

2 What changed as a result of the project?

    Change / new procedures being implemented

3 What resources were brought together for the project?

C-in Cross Practise Group
- Personnel

4 What sequence of activities was involved?

Courses / Meetings / Presentations

5 What was the timespan?

Ongoing

6 Who was responsible for the project?

Myself

FEEDBACK

Your response to this activity will depend on the particular nature of the project you were thinking of, but you should have been able to answer all, or almost all, of the questions. If you couldn't, are you absolutely sure it was a project? Check through the characteristics again.

What does a project manager do?

This is how some project managers described their role:

You are the driving force behind the project. It becomes the most important thing in your life and you have to transmit your energy and commitment to your team.

A project manager needs sufficient technical knowledge to understand the implications of every part of the project and the managerial ability to co-ordinate the different elements.

Managing a project is like keeping ten balls in the air at once whilst walking a tightrope.

It's a question of keeping one eye on the big picture and another on the day-to-day details.

The four key aspects of the project manager's role are:

- planning, organizing and co-ordinating
- monitoring and controlling
- leading
- communicating

PLANNING, ORGANIZING AND CO-ORDINATING

Every project is unique, with its own objectives, timescale and budget, and every project needs its own plan. As a project manager you have to work out what resources you need and how you are going to use them to achieve the necessary outcomes. You have to organize things so that the right people are available to do the right tasks at the right time. Your role as co-ordinator is crucial. You are probably the only person who knows everything that is going on and the significance of the separate elements.

MONITORING AND CONTROLLING

It is up to the project manager to keep the project running on the right lines. This means monitoring:

- costs
- schedules
- quality

You won't be an expert on every process involved in your project, but you must know enough to recognize when things are going wrong. Monitoring and controlling also means knowing when you need to step in and take corrective action – and when the best thing to do is to let your team sort the problem out.

LEADING

Projects involve bringing together people with different skills and experience and focusing their efforts on a particular goal. In order to do this you will need to inspire and motivate your team. There are many styles of leadership, from the authoritarian to the democratic. Project management requires a certain flexibility of approach. Depending on the people you are leading and the situation you are in, there will probably be times when you give a large degree of control to your team members, and other times when you have to take unilateral decisions.

COMMUNICATING

Some people say that this is the most important aspect of a project manager's task. Communication involves talking to:

- the project sponsors
- the project team
- the outside world

You must establish excellent communications with the project sponsors, who commissioned the work in the first place, to make sure that you share an understanding of what is to be achieved and the progress you are making towards your goal.

You must brief the members of your project team on what you want them to do – and keep the lines of communication open so that you are aware of any difficulties or breakthroughs. Since the individuals on your team will have different areas of expertise, it is likely that you will have to master some new forms of jargon so that you can ask the right questions and understand the answers.

You may also have to explain the project to people who are not directly involved in it. This could involve talking to other managers in your organization who are affected by your activities, or being interviewed by the press about what you are trying to achieve.

WHAT MAKES A GOOD PROJECT MANAGER?

Use the next activity to assess how well equipped you are at the moment to fulfil the role of project manager.

ACTIVITY 3

For each of the following statements, put a cross on the line to indicate your current position.

■ I can devise a complex and workable plan

I am confident   I need to
of my skills   develop my
in this area   ✕   skills in this area

■ I can implement a plan, work to schedule and stay within a budget

I am confident   I need to
of my skills   develop my
in this area   ✕   skills in this area

■ I know when I can leave people to get on with things and when I must step in

I am confident   I need to
of my skills   develop my
in this area   ✕   ✗   skills in this area

■ I know what and how to communicate in different situations

I am confident   I need to
of my skills   develop my
in this area   ✕   skills in this area

■ I can motivate other people to share my own priorities and values

I am confident   I need to
of my skills   develop my
in this area   ✕   skills in this area

■ I know how to get other people to do things right first time

I am confident   I need to
of my skills   develop my
in this area   ✕   skills in this area

■ I am prepared to vary my management approach to achieve my objectives

I am confident   I need to
of my skills   develop my
in this area   ✕   skills in this area

FEEDBACK

You probably decided that you were stronger in some areas than others. All these skills will be discussed in the workbook and you will have the opportunity to develop the aspects of project management where you feel less confident. Your answers to this activity will provide a useful guide to the areas in which you need to concentrate your efforts.

WHAT'S SO SPECIAL ABOUT PROJECT MANAGEMENT?

Many of the skills that a project manager needs are also required in everyday process management. A process manager must be able to organize, monitor, motivate – and communicate with – other people. The difference with project management is the **degree** to which these skills are needed.

A process is ongoing and your role as a process manager is to maintain stability. Most things that go wrong have happened before and you can use your experience, and the experience of those around you, to put them right again. If you have any weaknesses as a communicator or an organizer, the chances are that your colleagues will be aware of them and – to a certain extent – be prepared to compensate for your shortcomings. A process has its own momentum and, unless you are seriously underperforming, will probably carry you along with it.

A project, on the other hand, only happens once. You are dealing with a new situation and may be working with a particular group of people for the first time. You are using a unique combination of resources and working against deadlines. Although you will probably be familiar with many of the tasks you are managing, others will be new to you. What is more, your professional reputation is riding on the success of the project – and that success can be measured precisely against the criteria that were laid down at the start. Finally, since projects are concerned with innovation and change, you may encounter quite a bit of hostility directed towards your activities. In these circumstances, any mistake or error of judgement you make is going to be noticed.

Some people thrive on the pressures involved in project management. They find that the sense of ownership, the need to lay careful plans – and the way they have to find creative solutions when problems are encountered – brings out the best in them. Many senior managers also like the way that people perform when they are working on projects, which is why some organizations are running an increasing amount of their activities on these lines.

What happens in a project?

At the beginning of this workbook, we said that a project starts with an idea. It could also be argued that a project actually starts when the **need** for an idea is recognized. This can happen when an organization realizes that it has a problem of some kind, such as falling sales figures, an aggressive competitor, inadequate accounting procedures, high staff turnover or perhaps a poor health and safety record. Once the problem is recognized, alternative solutions can be considered and evaluated in a feasibility study, and a particular course of action, which may take the form of a project, be recommended.

ACTIVITY 4

Think back to the project you analysed in Activity 2. Was it set up to solve a problem? If so, what was the problem?

Increasing RAF persons

FEEDBACK

Many projects quickly gather their own momentum and are viewed as completely positive developments, not as reactions to a problem. However, unless a project meets a genuine need, it is unlikely to succeed. Even the Apollo Project started as a response to a problem. It was the United States' answer to the USSR's achievement of putting the first human into space.

THE PROJECT LIFE CYCLE

Once a project has been agreed upon, it goes through a series of stages:

1 Project start-up: what are we going to do?
2 Planning and organization: how are we going to do it?
3 Implementation: how well are we doing?
4 Conclusion and evaluation: how did it go? (and how could we do it better next time?)

Every project, whatever its size, goes through these stages.

ACTIVITY 5   B2, G2, G3

Think of a small project you have been involved in. What happened at the various stages? — *office move*

1 Project start-up

— meeting – setting deadlines / costs staff req's etc

2 Planning and organization

section need has ligns to work to liasia with I.T. removal from

3 Implementation

—

4 Conclusion and evaluation

FEEDBACK

Your answer may have something in common with the small project in the following example:

Project: Rearranging the office

1 Project start-up: The head of department decides it would be worth rearranging the furniture in the office and setting up a meeting area in the corner. She asks her deputy to take charge of the move and to get it done by the end of the month. She sets a budget of £2000 for any new furniture and equipment that is required.

2 Planning and organization: The deputy obtains a floor plan, measures furniture, asks staff about their need for working space and access to storage areas, etc., gets brochures about office tables, draws up plans and checks them with the head of department and staff, talks to IT department about moving computers on the network, orders new furniture, arranges the timetable for the move and asks people to help.

3 Implementation: The deputy oversees the clearance of desks, delivery of new furniture, movement of existing furniture and rewiring of network.

4 Conclusion and evaluation: The deputy takes everyone who has helped with the move out for lunch. The invoices for the new furniture are sent to Accounts for payment. Over the next couple of weeks, staff get used to the new arrangement and ask for some minor adjustments to be made.

Now we will take a look at what is actually happening at each of these stages.

PROJECT START-UP

This is the point at which big decisions are taken about the overall shape and direction of the project. If the wrong decisions are taken at the start, the project's chance of success are greatly diminished.

There is more than one way in which these decisions can be reached:

■ The project sponsors – the people who have the authority to set the project in motion and who are paying the bills – decide what needs to be done and then pass the project on to a manager who will carry out their wishes.

The managing director called me in and told me he'd got £5000 to spend on improving the IT system in the office. He gave me a catalogue in which he'd marked the type of software to go for – and could I please make sure that all the invoices were in before the end of the current accounting period.

In this situation, the project manager has hardly any autonomy at all. If the managing director has made the right decisions, everything may be all right. But there might be better ways to spend the £5000. Or it could be that more (or less) is needed to improve the IT system at this point. Or it could be that the project should be put off for six months until a new software package comes on the market.

■ The project manager has an idea for a project and persuades the sponsors to come up with the necessary resources.

I knew we needed to improve the IT system. I worked out where the problems were with the existing system, what we needed to put them right, the benefits that would result and how much it would all cost. I took the figures to the managing director and got his backing for the project.

This is a much healthier way of going about things. As long as the project manager has done the sums correctly, the project is likely to be a success. However, you will either have to have tremendous powers of persuasion, or a particularly enlightened sponsor, if you are to get everything you want for a project.

In practice, the big decisions are usually taken in consultation between the sponsors and the project manager. This may happen inside an organization, or during the negotiation of contracts between different organizations.

ACTIVITY 6

Think of a project you have worked on. — *NEW IAS SYSTEM*

1 What decisions were taken at the start-up phase?

— To look at site where possible comprised where is orgaris'd
— Time schedule

2 Who took these decisions?

3 At what point did you become involved?

4 Did any of the initial decisions about the project change after you were able to provide your input?

FEEDBACK

The start-up phase of a project often involves a great deal of negotiation. It is the time at which everyone comes to terms with what can actually be achieved with the resources available.

The more proactive you can be as a project manager at this stage, the better. Otherwise, you may find yourself committed to carrying out a project where the aims are:

- vague
- over-optimistic
- ill-informed
- downright inappropriate

If the project fails at a later stage because the wrong decisions were taken at the start, you may find yourself blamed for what has happened. It is much better to make a clear case for what you need right at the beginning.

The end of the first stage is marked by the production of an agreement between the sponsors and the project manager about what is going to be done. This document, which may be a formal contract or an internal memorandum, does not go into great detail about **how** the outcomes will be achieved. But it will state:

- what the sponsors will get
- when they will get it
- who will be involved
- what resources will be involved
- how much it will cost
- the general strategy

We will look again at the contents of this document at the end of the section.

PLANNING AND ORGANIZATION

ACTIVITY 7

Imagine you are organizing a transcontinental expedition by Land Rover. List six tasks you might have to do at the planning and organization stage:

1 THE RIGHT PEOPLE
2 GOOD BACK UP
3 COST
4 CONTINGENCY PLANS IF BREAKDOWNS / SICKNESS
5 CORRECT EQUIPMENT
6 TASKS FOR EACH TEAM MEMBER

FEEDBACK

Your list could have included: buying maps, getting visas, buying supplies, getting jabs, servicing (or buying) the Land Rover, buying spare parts, choosing the people who are coming with you, getting travellers cheques, planning your itinerary, packing the vehicle. You may have thought of other things. The point is that you would do everything you could to prepare yourself for the journey ahead.

A project is very like an expedition. It is essential to:

- get the right equipment
- get the right team
- find out as much as possible about where you are going
- anticipate (and protect yourself against) any problems you may meet along the way

Do as much preparation as you can before you set off, because you may not have the time or opportunity later.

Once you know **what** you want to achieve in a project, you have to work out exactly **how** you are going to do it. The first thing to do is to break down the project into separate tasks which you can:

- arrange in a logical order
- schedule
- cost
- assign to different individuals

This is the stage at which many of the tools which are often associated with project management – such as flowcharts, PERT diagrams and Gantt charts – come to the fore. Section 3 of this book explores how to use them.

At the planning stage, you are getting everything into position so that the project can run smoothly. You may be:

- appointing a project team
- writing briefing notes
- holding preliminary meetings
- assembling equipment
- working out your detailed budget

You must also set up the systems that you will use to monitor costs, schedules and quality.

IMPLEMENTATION

Now the project is actually underway. This is the time at which the maximum number of people are involved. The building is under construction, the training package is being written or the television advertisements are being shot.

Your role now is to monitor and control what is happening. The key elements to watch are time, cost and quality. It is very easy – and dangerous – for the project manager to become so involved in the action at this stage that the original purpose and direction of the project are lost. You must maintain some distance from what is happening around you, so that you can keep in touch with the big picture and understand the significance of any deviation from your plans. Section 4 of this book discusses techniques you can use to monitor and control your project during the implementation stage.

CONCLUSION AND EVALUATION

This is what happens after you deliver the results of your project. Your main concern at this moment will be with the reception that it gets. Haynes[1] writes that

The goal of project management is to obtain client acceptance of the project result.

It may be that the results of your efforts are greeted with universal acclaim. Or there may be a few small teething problems to sort out in the early days.

At the end of a project, you should also make your own evaluation of how things have gone. This may involve identifying:

- staff skills
- mistakes not to be repeated
- tools and techniques that were valuable
- things you would do differently another time

ACTIVITY 8

Think about a project you have been involved in. Note down four lessons that you learned from it.

1 ALLOW TIME
2 DONT BE AFRAID TO CHANGE THINGS
3 MAKE SURE THE RIGHT PEOPLE ARE IN THE TEAM.
4 DON'T ASSUME ANYTHING

FEEDBACK

The lessons that you learn from a project are probably the most valuable things that you take away from it. You will be able to use this experience to improve your performance as a project manager the next time around.

Resources

Everyday process management is often represented by a simple diagram:

Inputs → Process → Outputs

The inputs are materials, people, equipment, premises, energy and other resources which are needed for the process to take place. The process is how you go about doing it. The outputs are what you are manufacturing or producing.

A market gardener, for example, might apply the diagram like this:

Inputs	→	Process	→	Outputs
seeds		planting		tomato plants
compost		watering and feeding		
seed trays		transplanting		
flower pots				
fertilizer				
irrigation system				
greenhouse				
gardener's wages				
electricity				

ACTIVITY 9   B2.1, G1

Fill in the diagram for a process which takes place regularly in your organization.

Inputs	→	Process	→	Outputs
LETTER		INTERVIEW		POMMEST

FEEDBACK

You may have found it relatively easy to fill in the output and process columns, but more difficult to decide how much to include under inputs. In process management it is sometimes difficult to know how much the assets or supporting infrastructure of the organization contribute to the process.

The same diagram can be used to represent project management. Because a project starts with a clean slate, with no resources allocated to it, it is possible to be much clearer about the inputs, or resources, that are needed.

TYPES OF RESOURCE

Resources can take many forms. The main categories to consider are:

- **People**   People are often considered the most important resource in a project – you need to think about their experience, skills, energy and personal qualities
- **Finance**   This is necessary for any project – you need to consider the money which is needed at different stages of the project to pay suppliers and the project personnel
- **Time**   This is not always considered as a resource, but has a large effect on what you can achieve
- **Information**   This includes information about processes, products, markets, risks, etc.
- **Equipment**   This includes machinery, vehicles, computers, etc.
- **Materials**   These are consumed by the process
- **Services**   These could include use of premises and office services, also transport, accommodation, etc.
- **Energy**   Power and light are more important in some types of project than others

ACTIVITY 10

Now list the resources needed for a project you have worked on:

■ People

■ Finance

■ Time

■ Information

B2.1, G1

■ Equipment

■ Materials

■ Services

■ Energy

Which of these resources had to come out of the project budget? Circle them.

FEEDBACK

The more items you circled on the list, the more control the project manager probably had over the inputs to the project.

TIME, COST AND QUALITY

If you ask the people who are paying for a project what they would like to receive at the end of it, they will probably describe outputs which are:

- available quickly
- cheap
- perfect

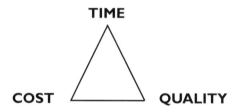

This triangle of time, cost and quality is something that every project manager has to juggle with. Sometimes, in order to maximize one aspect, you have to compromise on one or both of the others.

ACTIVITY 11

What conflicts between time, cost and quality can you see in each of the following cases?

1 'If we needed to get the building open to the public by the start of the tourist season, I could see that we were talking about the contractors working overtime for the next eight weeks.'

2 'I told the MD that if he insisted on hardwood floors instead of carpet in the new boardroom he would have to increase my budget.'

3 'There was no way that I could get a customized training package designed and written by the end of the month but I could certainly arrange for outside trainers to come in and give an off-the-peg course.'

FEEDBACK

In case 1, there is clearly a conflict between time and cost. In 2, the choice is between quality and cost. In 3, there is a conflict between time and quality. Remember that 'quality' does not just refer to a superior product but is also a measure of 'fitness for purpose'.

You can often save time in a project if you are prepared to spend more money – by increasing the number of people involved or using better equipment. Unfortunately, you can't usually save money by spending more time. If a project becomes extended over its due dates, other costs tend to accumulate.

The diagram which shows the transformation of inputs into outputs is a reminder that the quality of what comes out of a process is, to a large extent, governed by what goes in. In other words, you can't make a silk purse out of a sow's ear. The relationship between outputs and inputs is starkly obvious in project management – and it is therefore essential to specify exactly what you need in order to produce outputs which will satisfy your clients.

ACTIVITY 12

Think of a small project you would like to take charge of within your own department. What resources would you like to have at your disposal, given a completely free hand? Then lower your sights and think what resources you could actually manage to do the job with, at a pinch.

Project: Resources	Wish list	Basic list
People		
Finance		
Time		
Information		
Equipment		
Materials		
Services		
Energy		

FEEDBACK

The negotiations which take place at the start of a project are concerned with establishing exactly what resources are necessary to achieve the outputs which are required at the end of the project. You must be able to justify all the resources you require.

SETTING THE GROUND RULES

At the end of the start-up phase of a project, we said that an agreement will be drawn up between the sponsors and the project manager. This is known as the **Terms of Reference**. It sets the direction for the project, describes what you are going to do and the resources with which you can do it.

ACTIVITY 13

Put yourself in the place of a project sponsor. Think of a building or decorating job you would like to have done on your own home. Make some notes about the details you would want to agree with the people you employ to do it. Which aspects of the job would you want to control?

_____

_____

_____

_____

_____

_____

_____

_____

_____

FEEDBACK

Your answer will reflect your own priorities, and possibly your past experiences in this area, but you probably mentioned such aspects as:

- the improvement you hope to see when the work is finished
- time to complete the job
- cost
- the quality of the work
- the quality of the materials
- the disruption to your household
- what happens if something goes wrong

TERMS OF REFERENCE

In a business context, the Terms of Reference should include the following information:

Project sponsor

This is the individual or organization who has given authority for the project to go ahead and will accept (or reject) the outcomes. You may also have to refer to the sponsor if any details of the project have to be changed at a later stage of its development.

End-user of the project

This says who your final customers are. If the project involved writing a textbook, the end-users could be 'students on Advanced GNVQ courses in schools and colleges in the England and Wales'. If you were designing a new form of point-of-sale display for a confectionery manufacturer, they could be 'small- and medium-sized newsagents throughout the UK'.

Objectives

Objectives provide direction and motivation and make detailed planning of priorities possible. You can read more about setting objectives in other workbooks, but the most important thing to bear in mind is that an objective should be SMART:

- **S**imple
- **M**easurable
- **A**chievable
- **R**ealistic
- **T**ime-related

For example, if your project was concerned with developing a new system for transporting goods from the factory to supermarkets across the country, an appropriate objective might be:

- to cut delivery costs by 15 per cent by the end of this financial year

Deliverables

These are what the project sponsor expects to get at the end of the project. Deliverables are what they are paying for. They could take the form of a building, a market research report, a new logo for the side of the company delivery vans – or just about anything else you can think of. Deliverables must be described in enough detail so that there is no room for argument later.

Scope

This is a definition of the boundaries of the project. It might give details of which people, departments, processes and existing products are affected. It is important to establish the scope at the beginning, or you may waste time doing unnecessary work as in the following example:

We were asked to do a report on the comparative costs of employing our own cleaners in the offices or getting the work done by contractors. What we were not told was that the company was not going to renew the lease on the top two floors of the building next year, so all our calculations were based on inaccurate floor areas.

Costs

At the start-up stage, you will not know exactly how much the project is going to cost. This figure represents the budget you are working inside. It should include an amount built in for contingencies.

Resources

This is an overall indication of the resources required for the project. At this stage, you won't know exactly what you will need, but you should be confident that you can produce the necessary outputs with these inputs.

Timescale

This will usually give the finish date for the project, and any significant milestones on the way. You may only be able to give approximate times for some of the stages which happen later in the project.

Strategy

This gives an outline of how you are going to achieve your objectives. It may mention any special techniques you are going to use and any recognized standards you will be following.

Risks and contingencies

It may be that your project is dependent on external circumstances which you cannot control. For example, you may have heard that there is about to be a change in legislation which could affect your activities. Or a particular type of material you need may be in short supply. In this case, you should mention these risks in the Terms of Reference. You should also say how likely you think they are to occur, and what you will do if they happen. If the project sponsors know from the start that you may have to change your method of working to keep in line with new legislation, or perhaps increase the budget to pay for essential supplies, they will be much happier to accept these changes later on.

Roles and responsibilities

This will not include a detailed description of the people who will be working on the project, but may identify key roles and decision-makers. If the project is taking place within an organization, it may also indicate the nature and extent of the support you will be receiving from other departments.

ACTIVITY 14

Now complete this section by writing your own Terms of Reference for a project you would like to work on within your own department. You may like to use the same project for which you specified resources in Activity 12.

■ Project sponsor

■ End-user of the project

■ Objectives

■ Deliverables

■ Scope

■ Costs

■ Resources

■ Timescale

■ Strategy

■ Risks and contingencies

■ Roles and responsibilities

Summary

Now that you have finished this section, you should be able to:

■ recognize a project and describe its characteristics
■ explain the essential differences between project and process management
■ describe the role of a project manager at different stages of a project
■ describe the qualities you need to develop as a project manager
■ outline your priorities at various stages of a project
■ identify the various categories of resources needed for a project
■ explain the relationship between time, cost and quality in a project
■ write the Terms of Reference for a project

Notes

[1] Haynes, M. (1989) *Project Management: From Idea to Implementation*, Kogan Page

Section 2 Projects in context

This section takes a step back from the day-to-day practicalities of project management and looks at the wider context in which projects happen. It starts by asking you to think about the forces in the outside environment which led to your project happening. The section goes on to discuss how projects fit into organizations and considers the legal, ethical and financial issues which may influence you.

When you have finished this section, you should have a deeper understanding of why projects are organized and resourced in the way they are. You should also be in a stronger position to argue for the resources that you need.

The outside environment

Projects are used to bring about change. They are used to concentrate effort and resources on particular outcomes which will make a difference to the world. Some projects, such as the Channel Tunnel, affect the lives of millions of people. Others, such as the rearrangement of the desks in an office, have a much more limited impact. But all projects bring about a change of some kind.

Changes do not happen arbitrarily. There is always some reason, and usually a collection of reasons, why a change is necessary. We will begin this section by looking at some of the forces for change in the outside environment.

There are four types of external pressure which can bring about change in an organization:

- **S**ocial forces
- **T**echnological forces
- **E**conomic forces
- **P**olitical forces

They are usually known as STEP forces, from the first letter of each word.

SOCIAL FORCES

These forces come from the society in which we live. They include changes in the way people behave and the attitudes that they hold, and the way that the population as a whole is made up.

ACTIVITY 15

What changes have you been aware of in the last ten years in relation to:

■ marriage and divorce?

■ the age of the population?

■ attitudes to personal health?

■ gender roles?

FEEDBACK

Your answers may be similar to these:

■ **marriage and divorce**   An increasing number of marriages appear to be ending in divorce
■ **the age of the population**   There is a growing number of elderly people in the country, who will in time need increasing support from the rest of the population
■ **attitudes to personal health**   People are becoming more interested in alternatives to the conventional health services
■ **gender roles**   Girls now outperform boys at school, and women are now much more likely to be the main breadwinner in the household, although they are still under-represented in the higher levels of management

Here is a selection of projects which owe their beginnings, at least in part, to these social forces:

- the opening of a children's restaurant where divorced fathers can take their families at weekends
- the development of a workplace crèche for single parents
- a 'Third Age' health campaign organized by a local health authority, with exercise classes and healthy eating information for the over-70s
- the development of a recruitment policy for people over 50
- the development and marketing of a range of aromatherapy oils
- a management development training scheme for women
- an employment project in which local employers and trainers get together to improve the job skills of young unemployed men

ACTIVITY 16

Now think of a current social trend which has struck you as being significant. Does it suggest any ideas for changes which could be made by your organization?

FEEDBACK

If you were able to answer this activity, you may have the germ of an idea for a project here. If you want to take it further, you will have to back up your plan with facts and figures about the social trend you have identified.

TECHNOLOGICAL FORCES

Many projects are a direct result of technological changes. Your organization may itself be contributing to the development of technology. Or there may be pressure on you to use new technology in order to compete with other organizations and meet changes in customer demand.

ACTIVITY 17

1   What changes in technology have you seen in your organization in the last two years?

2   What role, if any, did projects have in the introduction of new technology?

FEEDBACK

Compare your answer with these:

Our company started to advertise on the World Wide Web. I was involved in a project to set up a home page.

We finally upgraded the tills in our supermarkets so that they can read bar codes. There was a training project for all the sales staff to show them how to use the equipment. There was also a research project to investigate what management could do with all the new information.

We have put all our archives onto CD ROM. There was a project team set up to decide which records we should keep and which we should get rid of.

We have started manufacturing clothing which uses new dyes which change colour at different temperatures. The development of the product was taken on as a project and has now been integrated into our overall production.

ECONOMIC FORCES

All organizations are subject to economic forces. They include:

- increasing unemployment
- inflation
- price changes
- interest rate changes
- new sources of funding
- expansion in the economy

Economic pressures can exist on an international or national scale, or affect one region of the country more than others. They can affect an organization's costs and the markets in which it operates.

ACTIVITY 18

1   What are the principal economic forces which are affecting your organization at the moment?

2   Do they present opportunities or threats?

FEEDBACK

Compare your answers with these:

- the level of business rates we have to pay in our town-centre outlets: threat
- the cost of borrowing money to develop new products: just at the moment, an opportunity
- no great demand for wage rises because of fears of unemployment: opportunity
- the fact that we are competing with firms in SE Asia with much lower wage rates: threat
- a drop in the cost of materials: opportunity
- a drop in the disposable income of our customers: threat

Both threats and opportunities can provide the basis for new developments within an organization, which may be brought about by projects.

POLITICAL FORCES

Like economics, politics operates on an international, national and local level. Here are some examples of how political pressures can influence organizations:

The local council sold off its housing stock and had several million pounds in its coffers which it wanted to spend to improve amenities in the town. They decided to construct a new sports and leisure centre. It would be a large, visible project which would make a lot of people happy. We were fortunate enough to get the contract to build it.

Changes in food hygiene regulations meant that we had to upgrade our kitchens. We put together a project team who planned and supervised the work that had to be done.

The EU ban on British beef in 1996 meant that we had to look for new markets for our meat products. The sales director commissioned a report from a firm of market research consultants.

Since the Lottery Fund came into existence, we've had a lot of approaches from local organizations who are looking for matching funding for their projects.

ACTIVITY 19

1 Identify a political pressure on your organization.

_____

2 Is the source
   ❑ local?
   ❑ national?
   ❑ international?
3 Does the pressure come from:
   ❑ changes in taxation?
   ❑ changes in legislation?
   ❑ something else?   _____

FEEDBACK

Political pressures, like the other STEP forces, can provide both opportunities and threats.

You have looked at the four STEP forces and seen some of the ways in which they can provide impetus or support for projects. Now read these extracts from an article about a major project planned to celebrate the millennium.[1]

Dawn of a new world

Conveying the excitement of plants, and their contribution to our lives, is the purpose behind the Eden project, set in a disused chalk pit in Cornwall. Architecture – a huge kilometre-long serpentine glass house by Grimshaw, Anthony Hunt Associates and Ove Arup's – is part of the vision ...

The architectural challenge is formidable. As a 'world class idea' [Tim Smit, who is promoting the project, said] 'it needed a world class consultant team. I am a great fan of Waterloo International, and they were the guys I felt I wanted.' ...

The county's traditional industries such as fishing and tin mining may be under pressure or extinct, but tourism is very active. Enormous numbers of visitors already go to Heligan [another Cornish garden], and the 1 million visitors for Eden predicted by the Arup-produced business plan represent only a small proportion of the number of tourist nights spent in Cornwall.

Half of the £105 million needed, Ball hopes, will come from the Millennium Commission which has already received a bid, while grants from English Partnerships and the European Regional Development Fund – Cornwall has special status as a depressed area – are in the pipeline. With the Millennium Commission's stated interest in ecological projects ... together with the project's regeneration implications and its combination of leisure and serious intellectual research, it must have a good chance.

ACTIVITY 20

What social, technological, economic and political factors are working in favour of the Eden project?

■   social factors

■   technological factors

■   economic factors

■   political factors

FEEDBACK

You might have identified:

■   **social factors**   attitudes towards the environment, interest in major projects to mark the millennium, patterns of tourism
■   **technological factors**   architectural breakthroughs transferred from Waterloo International project
■   **economic factors**   decline in other industries in the county, activity of tourism industry, funding available from the Millennium Commission and other sources
■   **political factors**   status of Cornwall as a depressed are

Incidentally, shortly after the article you read was published, the Eden project received funding from the Millennium Commission.

ACTIVITY 21

Write notes for an internal memorandum which describes the STEP forces which are working in favour of a project you would like to see happen in your organization.

FEEDBACK

One of the requirements of the MCI's management standards is that you should be able to take account of trends and developments in your plans for resource use. Your work on the STEP factors in the environment should help you to do this.

Working within the organizational framework

There are some important differences between the ways that projects and organizations are managed.

Organizations are primarily concerned with the long run and with long term targets. Their prime objective is that of survival, of continued existence, and in order to achieve this they are often prepared to sacrifice their original aims or radically alter their form or structure. This survival is not a time-related goal but a continual one that runs in front of the organization like a standing wave on the bow of a ship.[2]

Complete the following table[3].

	Organizations	Projects
Timescale	long term	
Horizon	unlimited	
Objectives	continuing survival	
Outcomes	replicas or hybrids	

FEEDBACK

From the work you did in the first section of this book, you will have recognized that projects work on a short-term timescale and have a clearly defined horizon. Their objectives are completion and termination and their outcomes are unique and one-off.

An organization can use a project to help it achieve its goal of long-term survival. As you have seen, projects can provide an opportunity for an organization to change direction or even restructure itself. There is, however, always a certain tension between a project and its client organization.

TYPES OF PROJECT ORGANIZATION

There are three main forms of project organization:

- **Client-centred**   The project team is integrated into the client organization, working for the project on a part-time or informal basis. The project makes use of the organization's personnel, expertise and infrastructure. It probably shares the same premises.
- **Project-focused**   Here the project team is completely separate. It has its own resources, staff and premises and communicates through senior management.
- **Matrix project**   This is a compromise between the other two positions. Project team members report to a functional manager within the organization and also to the project manager.

There are advantages and disadvantages to each of these forms of project organization:

Client-centred

Advantages

- in tune with the organization's procedures
- in tune with the organization's objectives
- supported by resources of organization

Disadvantages

- the work of the project may take second place to the work of the organization
- reduced ability of project to bring about change, especially if change threatens the values or structure of the organization
- project manager has limited authority and control

Project-focused

Advantages

- full commitment of team to the project
- project manager has full control
- decisions can be taken quickly

Disadvantages

- no use made of resources within the organization
- incompatibilities may develop between the objectives and systems of the organization and project

Matrix project

Advantages

- project can draw on resources of organization
- incompatibilities less likely to develop between project and organization

Disadvantages

- conflicts of loyalties can develop in project team

The following activity outlines some questions you can ask in order to decide which form of project organization to choose.[3]

ACTIVITY 23

In order to complete this activity you will need to know, for a particular project, the project's

- desired outcomes
- planned duration
- planned cost

1   Does the project need special technology or special knowledge to reach these outcomes? If yes, add 2 points.

2   If you answered yes to question 1, does the client organization have this knowledge or technology? If yes, subtract 1 point.

3   Are project implementation costs large? If yes, add 2 points.

4   Is the planned project to have a long duration? If yes, add 1 point

5   Does the project involve a high level of risk? If yes, add 2 points.

Total of points =_____

FEEDBACK

5–7 points   Use project-focused organization

3–4 points   Use matrix organization

0–2 points   Use client-focused organization

You may find it instructive to consider whether any projects in which you have been involved in the past had an appropriate structure.

The senior management of the publishing company where I work decided that they wanted a new company logo. Instead of giving the project to the in-house design department, they hired an outside designer. What they got was an acceptable result, but no better and no worse than the design department could have come up with. It didn't cost very much to employ an outsider, since it wasn't a very big job. However, it caused quite a bit of resentment, as it looked as though the management did not recognize or value the talents of the people they had working for them.

The Board decided they would update the training procedures across the organization. They set up a project team with representatives from all departments, who were responsible for assessing the training needs and deciding how to meet them. The project went on for about a year and the results were not very satisfactory. The trouble was that there was a great variation in the level of experience and understanding of training issues. Everybody came at the problem with their own local issues and agendas and the project manager did not have the authority to get everyone dancing to the same tune.

ACTIVITY 24

How were the two projects above organized (client-centred, project-focused or as a matrix project)? And how should they have been organized?

	Was organized as	Should have been organized as
New logo	_____	_____
Training scheme	_____	_____

FEEDBACK

The new logo was produced by a project-focused organization. Since the skills were already there in the client organization and the project was quite limited, it might have been better to have gone for a client-focused organization.

In the second situation, a matrix organization was chosen. However, the lack of technical expertise, the long duration and, most importantly, the divided loyalties of the team, all suggest that a project-focused organization would have been more effective.

ALIGNING YOURSELF WITH YOUR CLIENT ORGANIZATION

Let's suppose that you are managing a project for a client organization. You may be employed on a long-term basis by the organization, or have been brought in on a limited contract specifically to manage the project. What do you have to understand about the organization in order to maximize the chances of success of your project?

Mission

We have seen that the overriding aim of an organization is its own continuing survival. Most organizations give a lot of thought to what it is they want to continue doing, and express this in their mission statement.

An organization is unlikely to sponsor a project which is completely incompatible with its mission statement, but there may be times during the life of a project when it is important to remember the overall context in which the organization is working.

I was commissioned to direct a series of documentaries for the TV company whose mission statement was 'Commissioning television programmes of distinction'. Early in the process, I got the opportunity to buy in some sensational archive footage which had never been shown before. It was going to be very expensive, but I knew it would create a great stir. The commissioning manager was nervous about the cost, but I reminded her that she was supposed to be providing programmes 'of distinction' and managed to win her round.

Strategy

An organization's strategy is its long-term plan. It may concern, among other things:

- the market it operates in
- the types of products or services it offers
- the level of investment it makes
- the type of technology it uses

Most projects are started in order to support the strategy of the organization. However, sometimes a project may begin to take a different direction.

I was involved with a project to develop new database software for a company whose strategy was to supply small business users in the UK with IT applications. We were well on the way to developing a brilliant product but it was much more versatile than most small businesses needed. This sophistication was reflected in the price and the level of training that the people who operated it required. Because our clients were committed to the small business market, they pulled the plug on the project.

Unless the organization you are working for is prepared to vary its strategy, you need to keep your project in line with its long-term plans.

Procedures

Every organization has its own ways of taking decisions, passing on information and arranging and regulating its activities. If your project is closely involved with the day-to-day working of the client organization, these procedures will matter a great deal to you. You need to find out what they are and how they can be used to work to your advantage. Even if your project is quite separate from the client organization, you may still find that you are affected:

I was asked to develop a new range of handmade knitwear for the fashion department of a major store. I brought the samples in and was hoping for a quick decision about which items they wanted me to take to the next stage. However, they wanted to keep the samples until the next full management meeting so that everyone involved could have their say. I had no choice but to agree, but this meant that my team of knitters was standing by with nothing to do for three weeks.

Culture

The culture of an organization is shown by its procedures, and also by its values and the way people who work for it behave. If the project team is in contact with the organization's employees, it is important that they recognize and respect the prevailing culture, even if they don't share it themselves.

I was employed on a project to write a training package for a hotel company. They wanted me to work in the main office. All the other women, from the top managers to the secretarial staff, came to work in smart suits, wearing lots of make-up. That's not my style – I tend to be much more casual in the way I dress. However, for the six weeks I was working for the company I made an effort to fit in. Perhaps it shouldn't have been necessary, but I know that it helped them to take me and my ideas seriously.

Hidden agendas

There are usually some political undercurrents within a client organization. There may be individuals who have their own private reasons to want the project to succeed or fail. The project itself may also not be quite what it seems:

Some years ago, I was asked to produce a training scheme which would develop the management potential of women within the organization. I soon discovered that, far from offering women a route into management, what the board really wanted was to have a high-profile scheme that would impress the female clerical staff, who were getting very bored and frustrated with their jobs and giving in their notice at an ever increasing rate. What the project was actually intended to do was to save the company money by reversing the high level of staff turnover.'

It is not a good idea to get involved in the politics of your client organization, but it is sometimes important to know who your potential friends and enemies are – and what the real significance of your project is for the organization.

ACTIVITY 25

An outside consultant has been appointed to run a project which will look at the use of IT throughout the organization you work for. The managing director has asked you to give the consultant all the help he needs and not to hold anything back. The day after the contract has been signed, the consultant asks you to come for an informal chat, off company premises.

You approve of the project and respect the integrity of the consultant who has been put in charge. If you really want to help the consultant make a success of the project, what would you tell him about your organization's:

■ mission

■ strategy

■ procedures

■ culture

■ hidden agendas

If you are managing a project in an organization with which you are not familiar, how are you going to get a similar level of information?

Managing change

You may find that some of the people who work for the organization which is sponsoring your project do not trust you. This has nothing to do with your personal qualities as a human being. It is because you, as a project manager, are seen as a bringer of change. And most people do not like change, especially when it is forced upon them.

Before we look at ways of overcoming resistance to change, it is useful to spend a little time thinking about the nature of change itself.

FORCE FIELD ANALYSIS

Kurt Lewin, a social scientist, put forward a theory that people and organizations act in the way they do because of the effects of opposing forces. Some of these forces push us in one direction, while others push us in the opposing direction. The result is a state of equilibrium, in which both sets of forces are exactly balanced.

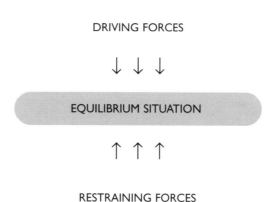

The forces can be anything which affect the situation, such as:

- people's attitudes
- costs
- quality
- information available
- resources available

ACTIVITY 26

Complete the following diagram. The current equilibrium is the poor time-keeping of the employees in an office. The driving forces are the pressures for the situation to improve and the restraining forces are the pressures which are preventing change.

DRIVING FORCES

_____

_____

_____

↓ ↓ ↓

POOR TIME-KEEPING

↑ ↑ ↑

_____

_____

_____

RESTRAINING FORCES

FEEDBACK

The forces you thought of may be similar to these:

Driving forces

- management's disapproval of latecomers
- performance-related pay
- pleasant working conditions

Restraining forces

- inadequate public transport
- inadequate car parking
- supervisor's toleration of the situation

If you want to change the situation, you have to take three steps:

1 Destabilize the equilibrium that currently exists
2 Move to a new position
3 Restabilize the new equilibrium

The way to destabilize the situation is to strengthen, or weaken, one or more of the forces which is producing the current equilibrium. In the situation in the last activity, this might have been done by **strengthening the driving forces** in one of the following ways:

- introducing a system of 'fines' for latecomers
- increasing the proportion of pay that is based on performance
- making further improvements to working conditions

or by **weakening the restraining forces** in one of the following ways:

- providing a mini bus to supplement public transport
- improving parking arrangements
- insisting that the supervisor takes a firmer line

Any of these actions could cause the equilibrium to move to a new position, although some would have more effect than others. Once equilibrium had been achieved again, it would be necessary to check the forces to make sure that the desired situation had been reached.

ACTIVITY 27

Now use force field analysis on a situation within your organization that you would like to change.

I   Identify as many driving and restraining forces as you can.

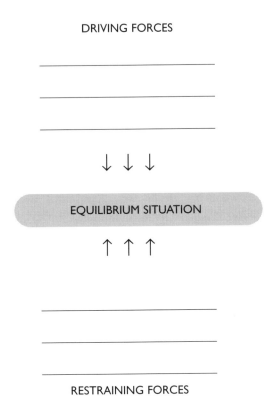

DRIVING FORCES

↓ ↓ ↓

EQUILIBRIUM SITUATION

↑ ↑ ↑

RESTRAINING FORCES

2   Which forces will you change to destabilize the situation?

FEEDBACK

It is likely that one of the restraining forces you identified was the attitude of some people in your organization. You may have decided to tackle this attitude directly to bring about a change, or to focus on some other driving or restraining force. In either case, you would have to contend with resistance.

OVERCOMING RESISTANCE TO CHANGE

People can react to change in a variety of ways. And the same individual will react to different types of change in different ways. Use the next activity to think about your own reactions to change.

ACTIVITY 28

Thinking about your own professional life:

1 Identify three changes which made you excited when you first heard about them

- _____
- _____
- _____

2 Now identify three changes which alarmed you when you first heard about them

- _____
- _____
- _____

FEEDBACK

Most people are excited by changes:

- in which they can see opportunities for themselves
- which make logical sense
- which seem to be better than the alternative of not changing
- which are brought about by individuals or agencies which have produced positive change in the past

The changes which alarm people are those:

- in which they fear they are going to lose something they value
- they can't understand
- they suspect contain errors or wrong assumptions
- they are unsure about the consequences
- where they distrust the person or agency who is promoting the change

The way to overcome resistance to change is to acknowledge people's concerns and to convert their resistance into commitment by:

- providing adequate information and explanation about what is happening
- involving people by giving them their own role and responsibilities in the change process

  For example, if you were in charge of a project to reorganize the arrangement of a suite of offices, you could overcome resistance from the people who used the offices by, for example:

- explaining why the changes were necessary
- asking people to work out their own needs for storage and working space
- offering a choice of new equipment

ACTIVITY 29

Consider the change which you analysed in Activity 27. What information and explanation would you give those involved?

What role could you offer them in the change process?

FEEDBACK

It can be time-consuming to overcome resistance to change. You may have to provide information or even training to enable people to participate in the change process in a meaningful way. It is not always practicable to manage change like this. However, if you have the resources available to you, it is almost certainly worthwhile.

Ethics

We will now look at a quite different type of issue which may affect how you resource and organize your project. Because projects take place outside the normal operations of an organization, they pose their own ethical dilemmas. There is certainly scope for unethical conduct in the relationship between the managers of a project, the client organization and any suppliers employed by the project.

ACTIVITY 30

Think about projects which have been sponsored by organizations you know. Were you ever aware of any of the following things happening? Tick any items which seem familiar.

- ❏ overcharging clients
- ❏ providing inaccurate accounts
- ❏ giving gifts or financial rewards in an attempt to influence business decisions
- ❏ delaying before settling suppliers' debts
- ❏ providing inadequate goods or services
- ❏ providing unsafe working conditions
- ❏ paying suppliers at too low a rate
- ❏ stealing other people's ideas
- ❏ falsifying information in order to win contracts
- ❏ causing environmental damage
- ❏ ignoring the confidential status of information
- ❏ spreading misleading information about competitors

FEEDBACK

Not all the items of this list are illegal, but they are all unethical and should clearly be avoided.

Many organizations would like to improve their ethical standards, but feel they can only make gradual changes. Because projects are outside the day-to-day work of an organization, and often have a high profile, they can provide a good place to start. The impetus can also come from the project manager to set high standards of ethics to the organization as a whole.

Here are some examples of ethical decisions made by project managers:

'We printed our report on recycled paper.'

'We made a point of not buying supplies from foreign countries who do not recognize human rights.'

'There were 20,000 information packs which had to be assembled at the end of our project. We made sure that the work went to an agency which paid decent wages.'

'We insisted that the contract contained provision for paying a refusal fee to any designer who provided sample drawings but whose work was not selected for the final design.'

'In our final report, we listed the names of all the individuals within the company who had helped us with our project.'

ACTIVITY 31

Are there any ethical issues which you feel particularly strongly about? If so, could you make a small step in this direction in the way you resource or organize a project?

FEEDBACK

It is possible that you may have more power to change things as a project manager than you do as an operational manager.

Financial issues

Workbook 10, *Effective Financial and Resource Management*, explores the financial aspects of resource planning in detail. Here, we will outline some issues which may have a bearing on whether your project is sponsored in the first place and how it will be funded.

An organization often has to make a choice between several different projects, only one of which it can afford to fund. These projects may involve doing:

■ completely different things, or
■ the same thing in different ways

One way to choose between projects is to work out a list of criteria of things which are important and then to rank each project against these criteria. This is much the same procedure that you would go through yourself when making any significant purchase.

ACTIVITY 31

What criteria would you consider when buying a house? List six points:

1

2

3

4

5

6

FEEDBACK

Your criteria might have included any of these: cost, maintenance costs, number of bedrooms, garden, location, age, state of repair, proximity to schools, shops or public transport.

Cost would almost certainly have been an important factor in your decision, but there may have been other criteria which had equal importance:

For me, it was absolutely essential to have a house that was near public transport and I was prepared to pay slightly over the odds for that.

The same kind of consideration can influence the choice of project.

ACTIVITY 32

Here is a list of criteria which might be important when choosing a project to build new premises. Think about your own organization. Which criteria would be more important to them? Rewrite the list in order of importance. Add any other criteria you think might also influence your organization's decision.

- cost   _____
- architectural merit   _____
- time before completion   _____
- space provided   _____
- energy saving design   _____
- use of local contractors   _____
- car parking   _____
- ▪   _____
- ▪   _____

FEEDBACK

Different organizations would have their own priorities here. For some, cost would be the overriding factor, while others might need to have a building that was ready quickly. You may notice that the elements of cost, time and quality are all important in this type of decision.

Once an organization has decided its priorities for a project, each candidate can be evaluated and ranked against them. In the following analysis, three projects (A, B and C) are evaluated. For each criteria, they are ranked as 1, 2 or 3, with 1 indicating the first choice.

	A	B	C
cost	3	1	2
time	3	2	1
space	2	1	3
architecture	2	1	3
energy saving	1	2	3
local contractors	1	3	2
car parking	1	3	2

Here, the best choice would probably be project B. It scores highly against the criteria at the top of the table, which are those which are most important to the organization.

LOOKING AT THE FIGURES

It is often necessary to look at the financial implications of projects in more detail. There are several ways of doing this for projects which are expected to bring a financial return to the organization.

Payback

This is a relatively simple calculation of how long it will take a project to pay back the initial capital which is invested in it. For example, if a company plans to spend £2000 on a new piece of equipment which will generate profits of £500 a year, the payback period would be:

$$\frac{\text{Implementation cost}}{\text{Annual profit}} = \frac{£2000}{£500} = 4 \text{ years}$$

When projects are compared in this way, the one with the shortest payback period is selected. The problem with this method is that it does not take account of any profit that arises after the project costs have been met. It also disregards the changing value of money, which can be crucial if large sums are involved.

Rate of return

Here, the annual profit is divided by the implementation cost and multiplied by 100, to give a percentage.

$$\frac{\text{Annual profit}}{\text{Implementation cost}} \times 100 = \frac{500}{2000} = 25\%$$

Here, the project with the highest rate of return would be chosen. This method has the same drawbacks as the payback method.

Net present value

If large amounts of money are involved, it is essential to take into account the fact that the value of money changes over time. You may be confident that a project will bring in an annual profit of £50,000 in five years time, but this £50,000 will be worth less, in the sense that it will buy less, than £50,000 today. The further in the future that profits are expected, the less they will be worth in today's terms. Net present value is calculated by converting all the future earnings of a project to their present value.

The following equation is used:

$$\text{Present value} = \frac{\text{Future value}}{(1+r)^n}$$

where n = number of years

and r = assumed interest rate or cost of capital

If you assume an interest rate of 10 per cent, the expression $(1+r)^n$ will represent:

$(1+0.1)^1 = 1.1$ after 1 year

$(1+0.1)^2 = 1.21$ after 2 years

$(1+0.1)^3 = 1.33$ after 3 years

$(1+0.1)^4 = 1.46$ after 4 years

(All figures correct to two decimal places.)

So, to calculate the net present value of a project costing £500 which would bring in the following profits:

Year number	0	1	2	3	4
Annual profit	−500	200	300	250	250

You must divide the expected profit in each year by the appropriate value of $(1+r)^n$.

$$\frac{200}{1.1} = 181.81 \quad \text{(year 1)}$$

$$\frac{300}{1.21} = 247.93 \quad \text{(year 2)}$$

$$\frac{250}{1.33} = 187.97 \quad \text{(year 3)}$$

$$\frac{250}{1.46} = 171.23 \quad \text{(year 4)}$$

You add up these figures to find out the total present value:

788.94

And subtract the original costs to find out the net present value:

$$788.94 - 500 = 288.94$$

ACTIVITY 33

1   Which would you choose, a project with a net present value of 15.00 or 23.00?
2   Would you sponsor a project with a net present value of −1.6?
3   Can you think of two ways in which you could increase the net present value of a project?

FEEDBACK

1   All other things being equal, the project with the higher net present value would be preferable.
2   No, because the capital costs would outweigh the discounted returns.
3   You could either reduce the costs, or shorten the timescale so that the profits came onstream earlier.

The legal framework

We will end this section with a brief reminder of the legal framework in which projects exist. Although you would not normally be expected to be a legal expert as a project manager, it is important to be aware of the areas in which you may need to get specialist advice.

ACTIVITY 34

Use this checklist to consider the legal issues relevant to your project.

❑ Planning permission from the local authority – for new buildings or change of use

❑ Health and Safety at Work Act 1974 – plus more recent EU directives on health and safety

❑ Contract law – if you are making contracts with your client organization or suppliers

❑ Environmental Protection Act 1994 – if your project might involve pollution or a nuisance to the public

❑ Sale of Goods Act 1979 – if you are introducing new goods onto the market

❑ Data Protection Act 1984 – if you are gathering data or using data for new purposes

❑ Sex Discrimination Acts 1975 and 1986, Race Relations Act 1976 – if you are employing people

❑ Employment Protection (Consolidation) Act 1978 if you are employing people

❑ Legislation which is specific to your own sector of industry

In this section you have considered many different issues which may affect how you set up and resource your project – and also how it is viewed by the organization which is paying for it. Use the final activity to apply what you have learned to a particular project you are involved in.

ACTIVITY 35

1 Look again at the Terms of Reference you drew up at the end of the first section. Is there anything you would like to add or change?

2 Use the insights you have gained from the section you have just completed to make notes for a presentation to support your proposals.

You may like to think about these points:

- driving and restraining forces
- the relationship between your project and the client organization
- how you will manage change
- ethical issues
- cost
- the legal framework

Summary

Now that you have finished this section, you should be able to:

- identify forces for change in the external environment
- choose an appropriate type of project for an organization
- align a project with the priorities of the client organization
- perform a force field analysis and identify ways of bringing about change
- overcome resistance to change
- recognize ethical issues relevant to project management
- take account of financial constraints on projects
- identify legal issues which affect project management decisions.

Notes

[1] Melvin, J., 'Dawn of a new world', *Building Design*, 26 January 1996
[2] Adapted from Baguley, P. (1995) *Managing Successful Projects: A Guide for Every Manager*, Pitman Publishing/Institute of Management
[3] ibid.

Section 3   Planning a project

In this section we get back to the practicalities of planning a project. You will think about putting a team together and deciding what other resources you need. You will also look at some of the many planning tools used in project management.

The section will help with the second stage of the project life cycle, when you do your detailed planning and organization. As your understanding of what is involved in project managment deepens, you may also find that you want to think again about some of the big decisions made at the start-up stage.

You will also find that the part of the section which covers building a team is relevant to the implementation and concluding stages of a project.

Building a team

Projects need people. One of your first tasks as project manager is to assemble a team of people with relevant skills who will help you achieve your objectives.

WHAT IS A TEAM?

A team is not the same as a group. A group of people may all be doing the same thing at once, but they are acting individually, not in co-operation. Imagine this situation:

A group of people in an office are quietly getting on with their own work when the door opens. 'Help! I've got to get 30 information packs ready for the managing director to take to Edinburgh in half an hour.' Immediately, the room is galvanized into action. Somebody clears the central table. Somebody else gets stacks of leaflets out of the cupboard. Someone else drafts a covering letter and prints out 30 copies. Another individual handles all the telephone calls coming into the room. Three people are soon collating leaflets into wallets while someone checks the contents and adds the letters. In 20 minutes, the packs are ready.

For twenty minutes, the group turned itself into a team. This happened because everyone understood the need to achieve a particular goal. They took on the variety of roles which were necessary for the task to be completed and co-operated to meet their objective.

In crisis situations, such as wars and disasters, teams can come together spontaneously and achieve great things. One of the reasons why some people enjoy team sports is that they experience a similar kind of commitment, co-operation and excitement at their achievements.

A project should not be a crisis, but you do need to assemble a team which can:

- share commitment to a common goal
- co-operate to achieve this goal
- take different functional roles
- sustain this behaviour for the life of the project

Not all teams can do this. You must give careful thought to whom you want on your project team.

PICKING THE TEAM

Your team must be able to perform the functional roles necessary for the project. A team to produce a textbook might include:

- an author
- a subject expert to check the facts
- an editor
- an administrator
- a graphic designer
- an illustrator
- a DTP operator

ACTIVITY 36

Think of a project you have worked on. What were the functional roles?

FEEDBACK

Sometimes one person fills more than one functional role, or one role is shared by several individuals.

In addition to their functional skills, your team members must also be able to work together as a team. This means that they should be able to:

■ make decisions
■ solve problems
■ co-operate with each other
■ use interpersonal skills with each other.

It is not necessary for everyone on the team to have these qualities to the same level. This would be impossible to achieve, and many experts say that the best teams are made up of people with differing personal styles and strengths.

The following chart gives the nine team roles identified by Belbin:[1]

Role	Team-role contribution	Allowable weaknesses
Plant	Creative, imaginative, unorthodox. Solves difficult problems.	Ignores details. Too preoccupied to communicate effectively.
Resource investigator	Extrovert, enthusiastic, communicative. Explores opportunities. Develops contacts.	Overoptimistic. Loses interest once initial enthusiasm has passed.
Co-ordinator	Mature, confident, a good chairperson. Clarifies goals, promotes decision-making, delegates well.	Can be seen as manipulative. Delegates personal work. Can provoke others.
Shaper	Challenging, dynamic, thrives on pressure. Has the drive and courage to overcome obstacles.	Hurts people's feelings. Lacks drive and ability
Monitor evaluator	Sober, strategic and discerning. Sees all options. Judges accurately.	to inspire others. Overly critical. Indecisive in crunch
Teamworker	Co-operative, mild, perceptive and diplomatic. Listens, builds, averts friction, calms the waters.	situations. Can be easily influenced. Somewhat inflexible.
Implementer	Disciplined, reliable, conservative and efficient. Turns ideas into practical actions	Slow to respond to new possibilities. Inclined to worry
Completer	Painstaking, conscientious, anxious. Searches out errors and omissions. Delivers on time.	unduly. Reluctant to delegate. Can be a nitpicker. Contributes on only a
Specialist	Single-minded, self-starting, dedicated. Provides knowledge and skills in rare supply.	narrow front. Dwells on technicalities. Overlooks the 'big picture'.

ACTIVITY 37

Imagine you are shipwrecked on a desert island with a group of eight other people. Your aim is to build a boat and escape. There is a boat-building manual on the island and materials are plentiful.

1 Whom would you like to be on the island with you?

2 Choose eight people whom you know personally or have worked alongside who will, with yourself, make up the perfect team. Which roles will they take in the team? Which team role will you take yourself?

Plant
Resource investigator
Co-ordinator
Shaper
Monitor evaluator
Teamworker
Implementer
Completer
Specialist

FEEDBACK

If you found this activity difficult, consider whether you are sufficiently aware of people's personal strengths and weaknesses. If you are putting together a project team which will work together closely, you may need advice from someone who is more confident about assessing other people. In a large project, you might think about getting applicants to meet as a group to see how they got on together. You might also consider using psychometric testing to help you assess applicants.

It is important to have a team of the right size. If the team is too large, people may feel that their skills are underused and less assertive individuals may feel that they are disregarded. Large teams can break down into factions and it may be hard to reach consensus. Creativity and problem-solving seems to happen better in small teams, which also show more commitment. It is, however, important to cover all the key functional roles. The most effective size for a project team seems to be from six to eight people.

TEAM DYNAMICS

Once you have picked your team, you must allow time for it to start acting as a team. Whenever a group of people is brought together, it goes through certain recognized stages:[2]

- forming
- storming
- norming
- performing
- mourning

Forming

The group comes together and starts to think about the task. At this point, members are sizing each other up and are very dependent on the leader. Some people may be hesitant to join in. People may waste time talking about irrelevant issues. Little work gets done at this stage.

How you can help: Give clear introductions. Make yourself visible as the leader. Provide opportunities for members to join in.

Storming

Arguments may break out. People may resist the validity of the task and may react emotionally against demands made of them. Sub-groups may emerge and there is defensiveness and ambivalence towards the leader.

How you can help: Recognize the conflict openly and give people opportunities to express themselves, showing that you value ideas even if the rest of the group does not. Encourage people to challenge each other constructively, not destructively.

Norming

People ask and give opinions. They feel able to express opinions. Plans are made. A sense of cohesion is emerging and the members start to identify with the group.

How you can help: Allow people time to begin to work together and make preliminary decisions.

Performing

There is strong orientation towards the goal. People have clear but flexible goals and are pragmatic towards the task. There is satisfaction in what the group has achieved.

How you can help: Let the group get on with things, joining in when appropriate.

Mourning

At the end of the task, people look for other tasks to do. They may not want to recognize that the group is over. The group's work is evaluated and some people may show extra enthusiasm for what it has achieved. Some people may want to make a rapid exit.

How you can help: Recognize that the group is coming to an end. Summarize what has been achieved and where to go from here. Allow time for goodbyes.

ACTIVITY 38

Use what you have just read about how groups behave to answer the following questions:

1   Would it be a good idea to invite your project sponsor to an early team meeting?

2   Assuming your team follows this pattern of stages, would you expect to have more or less day-to-day contact as the project progresses?

FEEDBACK

1   It would probably be a mistake to invite a sponsor to meet the team before it had reached the 'performing' stage. Earlier in the process, they may still be working out their roles and questioning the project. You also need to make yourself visible as the leader of the team.

2   If your team settles down and starts to 'perform' you can withdraw slightly, because they are less dependent on you as leader.

If possible, you should try to synchronize the 'performing' stage with the time when you will need the greatest activity from your team. This is usually the implementation stage of a project. You must allow the team time and opportunity to come together and work through the preceding stages beforehand.

Estimating

Next, we will look at quite a different aspect of planning — how to work out in advance the amount of time and money you will need for your project.

ACTIVITY 39

We all use estimates in daily life, often without thinking about them very much. How would you go about estimating the following things? Concentrate on the **method** you The figures themselves are irrelevant here.

1   how long it takes you to have a bath and wash your hair:

2   how long it takes to assemble the second of two shelving units you bought in flat packs:

3   the cost of a meal in a restaurant you last visited five years ago:

4   how long it takes to go into town and do some shopping:

FEEDBACK

1   You know how long it has taken you to do these things in the past. You would base your estimate on historical data.

2   You would use historical data (how long it took you to assemble the first unit) but expect to complete the second in less time, now you know what you are doing.

3   You would remember roughly how much you spent at the restaurant when you visited it previously, and expect prices to have gone up since then. You would therefore be basing your estimate on historical data with an adjustment for inflation.

4   This would depend on how much shopping you wanted to do. You would know that the journey into town would take a fixed time (based on historical data) and would add a variable amount of time, depending on how many shops you thought you were going to visit.

These basic methods are also used in a work context to work out rough estimates of:

■   historical data – for example, price paid for materials or services in the past

■   historical data adjusted for familiarity with the task – for example, time you allow for experienced workers and new recruits to complete the same job

■   historical data adjusted for inflation – for example, prices paid in the past, or to be paid in the future

■   combination of fixed and variable amounts – for example, any bill which includes a fixed charge (such as a call-out charge) plus an extra amount based on the time and materials involved

The accuracy with which you can make estimates will depend very much on your knowledge and experience. You are probably familiar enough with your own job to make a fairly reliable guess at how long it will take you to complete any particular task it involves.

However, projects are, by definition, unique. They are made up of a series of activities, some of which you will understand and some of which may be completely new to you. Even if you are familiar with every separate task involved in a project, you will never have encountered them in exactly this combination, designed to achieve these particular objectives.

In the early stages of a project, when big decisions are being made about timings and costs, it is impossible to make accurate estimates. You simply do not have the information. All you are able to do is to use your experience of similar situations in the past, adjust them for the factors you think are different this time around, and make the best estimate you can. In most industries, there are some well known 'rules of thumb' which can give a general idea of costs. The first estimates you make may be out by up to plus or minus 30 per cent. Incidentally, it is important that the people to whom you are giving your first estimates are aware of this potential for error.

DEFINITE ESTIMATES

When you reach the planning stage of a project, you are in a much better position to make more accurate estimates. At this point, the outcomes of the project will have been decided in much more detail. You can now begin to work out some serious figures. Your estimate of costs may contain these elements:

- labour (including fees for people like yourself who are working throughout the project and people who are paid by the week, day or hour)
- equipment (which may be hired, leased or bought for the project)
- materials
- overheads (such as insurance, consultancy fees, rent, phone bills)
- an allowance for inflation (if the project is taking place over an extended period of time)
- a contingency allowance

The contingency allowance will normally be about 5 per cent. This is not included to allow for any changes in the scope of the project, or for any errors you have made in your calculations. The purpose of a contingency allowance is to cover unforseeable events, such as errors made by people involved in the project or large changes in interest rates.

ACTIVITY 40

Consider a project you might manage yourself in the near future. Using the following headings, make a list of the items you would include in your estimate.

■ labour

■ equipment

■ materials

■ overheads

■ allowance for inflation (if relevant)

■ contingency allowance

FEEDBACK

You may have decided that some items (such as overheads) would not be charged directly to the project but would be carried by the organization in which it takes place.

Accurate information about costs can now be gathered from a variety of sources. You might use:

- catalogues
- industry standards
- conversations with suppliers
- quotations from suppliers
- records of previous projects
- trade and government indices
- your own experience
- the experience of colleagues

ESTIMATING TECHNIQUES

Several formulae have been worked out which will allow you to apply data about costs to your own project.[3]

Factorial estimating

By studying the records of previous projects, you may be able to work out relationships between the cost of different elements. These are a more sophisticated version of the 'rules of thumb' derived from people's experience of particular types of work.

Learning curves

Performance improves with practice. The first time you do a task, you are finding out what needs to be done and how to go about it. The second time, you will be faster. It has been calculated that, for most tasks, people improve their speed by between 80 and 90 per cent each time the number of repetitions doubles. If it takes one hour to do a task the first time, it will take, on average:

1×0.8 hours to do it the second time
$1 \times 0.8 \times 0.8$ hours to do it the fourth time
$1 \times 0.8 \times 0.8 \times 0.8$ to do it the eighth time,
and so on.

ACTIVITY 41

Sketch out the learning curve on a graph. What do you think is going to happen to the line as the number of repetitions increases?

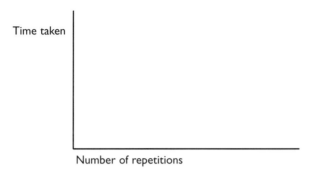

FEEDBACK

The line flattens out. Because you have to double the number of repetitions each time to achieve the same increase in speed, this figure soon approaches a steady value.

You have to remember that the learning curve is based on mean values and that individual performance will vary. And different tasks have different shapes of learning curve. However, if you have enough data, you can use this principle to estimate how long people are going to take to complete a task once they become accustomed to it.

It also follows that, if you have a short task which must be repeated many times, it may be worth giving it to inexperienced (and possibly cheaper) individuals and allowing them time to improve their performance. If you have a longer task, which only needs to be performed once or twice, there may not be time in the project schedule for an individual to move along the learning curve and you would be advised to find someone more experienced to do the work.

Building up and winding down

People do not achieve peak performance all the time. It is very easy to base estimates on how long a job will take on the amount of work people can get done when they are working at their best. In practice, it has been found that in the first 20 per cent of time that a job takes, people work up from doing nothing to their peak rate of activity in a linear manner. The same thing happens in reverse during the final 30 per cent of the time a job takes.

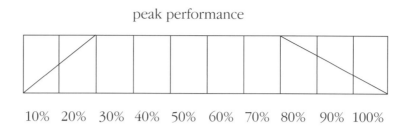

peak performance

10% 20% 30% 40% 50% 60% 70% 80% 90% 100%

You can see from the diagram that people only achieve half their peak output in the first 20 per cent and last 30 per cent of a job. Over the whole job, they will only achieve 75 per cent of what they could manage if they were working at their top rate all the time. This means that you may have to increase the time you have allowed for a job if you have assumed that people will be working at peak performance all the time. If the job must be completed in a fixed amount of time, you may have to increase the number of people you assign to do it.

BEING REALISTIC

When you are preparing a budget or a schedule, it is very tempting to be overoptimistic about what you can achieve and come up with figures and dates that you think the project sponsor would like to hear. It is much better to produce estimates you know you can stick to.

However, work has a tendency to expand to fill the time available. Expenditure can also expand to take up the budget available. If you tell people that you expect them to work at anything less than peak performance, you may demotivate them. Most project managers build in some safety margins into their plans, which they do not advertise to their team. The degree to which you do this will depend on how democratic and open you are with your team. You may find that people's commitment and sense of personal responsibility increases when you trust them with the real picture.

Specifying and prioritizing resources

When you are selecting resources, four factors are important:

- quality
- price
- delivery
- service

Quality

Resources must do the job for which you need them, but there is no point in spending project funds on equipment or materials that have higher specifications than you need.

Price

The price of a resource may include its purchase price and any running or maintenance costs. For example, if you were choosing a laser printer, you would have to take into account the cost of replacement cartridges. Price is also affected by volume. If you know you are going to use a large amount of a particular material over the life of a project, make arrangements to buy in bulk at the beginning.

Delivery

This may be the time it will take for the resource to be delivered, and also the reliability of the delivery time.

Service

This can include information or advice that is provided with a resource and any maintenance agreements. This can be significant if you are using types of equipment or materials with which you are unfamiliar.

A decision about any resource can be divided into two stages:

1   What do you need?
2   Where are you going to get it?

WHAT DO YOU NEED?

You can use a variation on a technique introduced earlier in the book to identify and prioritize your needs.

Use these headings to identify your needs of a particular resource. (You will probably have more than one point to make under some of them.)

■ **quality**

■ **price**

■ **delivery**

■ **service**

Next, list your requirements in order of priority. Draw a line underneath the section of the list which represents the aspects of the resource which are absolutely essential to you.

Here is a list drawn up by a project manager who was thinking about her requirements for an office chair:

swivel
arms
cost less than £150

_____

delivered next week
guaranteed for a year
black

You can now match these specifications against those provided by possible suppliers.

WHERE ARE YOU GOING TO GET IT?

You may have a choice between several different suppliers. You must decide how closely each supplier can meet your specifications.

		Supplier		
		A	**B**	**C**
	swivel	✓	✗	✓
Essential	arms	✓	✓	✓
	< £150	✗	✗	✓
	next week	✗	✓	✗
Desirable	1-year guarantee	✓	✓	✗
	black	✗	✓	✓

Here, Supplier C is the only possibility, because they are the only ones to meet the requirements in the essential part of the list.

An alternative method, which we used earlier in the book, is to rate alternative suppliers against each other for their ability to meet your various requirements.

You may have a choice of whether you use a supplier you have used before, or one that is new to you. You will have to make an assessment of:

- the risk of using an untested source
- the extra effort that a new supplier may be prepared to put in for a new customer
- the extra effort that an old supplier may be prepared to put in to keep your custom

WHICH RESOURCES?

It may not be possible for you to spend time preparing exact specifications for all the resources you need for your project. One method you can use to decide where to concentrate your efforts is to prepare an ABC analysis.

Here is a list of what somebody would expect to buy for an informal office party to celebrate a secretary's birthday. It is arranged in order of cost, with the most expensive categories at the top.

wine
beer
nuts
mineral water
crisps
paper cups
champagne
balloons
birthday card

(Champagne is near the bottom of the list because, although it is an expensive item, the person planning the party is only going to buy one bottle.) The next step is to divide the resources into three groups:

A greatest importance
B medium importance
C least importance.

You may decide to do this entirely on grounds of cost. The standard ABC analysis is based on the principle that, in most enterprises, 20 per cent of resources account for 80 per cent of the total spending. The items which make up this 20 per cent go into your A category, which is where you should make the greatest effort to establish and meet your specifications.

However, there may be other considerations to take into account. In the list for the office party, the birthday card is rated last, because it will cost the least. It may be absolutely crucial to the success of the party that an appropriately witty birthday card is chosen for the occasion. This item should therefore be added to the 'A' list of resources.

ACTIVITY 43

Do an ABC analysis on the types of resources you would need for a small project. Are there any items for which the specifications are so important that they must be moved up the list of priorities?

ABC analysis, like most tools, will not provide all the answers. Use your own specialist knowledge and the knowledge of your colleagues.

Planning tools

There is a group of planning tools which have a close association with project management. These are:

- work breakdown structure
- flowcharts
- PERT diagrams
- Gantt charts

With the help of these tools, you can get from the point where you only have a general idea of what a project involves to the preparation of detailed schedules.

WORK BREAKDOWN STRUCTURE

When you begin a project, you know the outcome you must achieve, but you may not know **how** you are going to achieve it. This is normal. Projects consist of a sequence of different activities. Although you may have specialist knowledge of some of these activities, you are very unlikely to be an expert in all of them.

You need to break the project down into smaller elements, which you can then cost, schedule and control. You should do this in several stages. First of all, divide the project into its major phases.

If your project involved producing a catalogue for a specialist shop, these phases could be:

- preparation
- printing
- mailing

ACTIVITY 44

Work out the phases for a project you might manage in the future.

FEEDBACK

If you can't do this, don't be alarmed. You can get the information from someone who has managed a similar project in the past.

Next, break down the phases into separate activities it involves. You may have to consult other members of the project team at this point to find out what these activities are.

For the first stage of the production of the catalogue, the activities might be:

Preparation

- Decide on items to go in catalogue
- Write entries
- Check entries
- Design
- Typeset
- Get photographs taken
- Prepare cover

Of course, printing and mailing can be similarly broken down.

ACTIVITY 45

Work out the activities for one phase of the project you were thinking about in Activity 44. For the sake of **this** activity, choose a phase with which you are reasonably familiar.

FEEDBACK

You may still be thinking at quite a general level, but your list of activities should be complete.

The last stage is to break these activities down into individual tasks. Here you will almost certainly have to take advice from people with specialist knowledge of particular parts of the project.

The tasks for the first activity in the preparation of the catalogue could be:

Decide on items to go in catalogue

- Visit shop
- Ask owner's views
- Analyse sales figures
- Prepare list
- Check with owner
- Amend list.

Similarly, all of the other preparation activities can also be broken down, and represented in a diagram if necessary.

A description of the characteristics of individual tasks is shown below.[4]

Tasks should:

- Be measurable in terms of cost, effort, resource and time
- Result in a single verifiable end product
- Have clear start and end dates
- Be the responsibility of a single person

ACTIVITY 46

Work out the tasks for one activity of your own project.

FEEDBACK

If you could not move straight from activities to tasks which have the characteristics described above, it may be that you need to insert another level in the structure first. Some projects can have up to five levels in the work breakdown structure.

Once you have divided the whole project up into tasks, these tasks can be described separately. The following information may be necessary:

- description of task

- anything that has to happen first
- outcome
- resource requirements, with costs
- skills needed
- responsibilities
- time

In a complex project, it may be necessary to record this data on standardized task-definition forms.

FLOWCHARTS

Flowcharts are an excellent way of discovering what a project actually involves and for working out which activities, or tasks, have to happen before others. The basic principles of flowcharts are very simple.

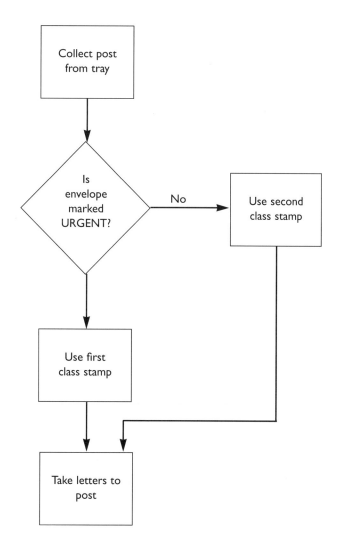

A rectangle indicates a process and a diamond indicates a point at which a decision must be taken and two courses of action are possible. Software programs are available which enable you to draw up flowcharts very quickly. You will find that these contain other symbols, including some to indicate start and finish points, documents and points at which control passes from one individual to another. The sophistication of your flowchart will depend on complexity of your project.

ACTIVITY 47

Sketch a flowchart to describe a process with which you are familiar.

FEEDBACK

If you are not used to preparing flowcharts, you may have found this more difficult than you expected. Flowcharts force us to think very logically about the relationship between different activities.

You may find it helpful to use flowcharts in conjunction with your work breakdown schedule.

PERT DIAGRAMS

Project Evaluation and Review Technique (PERT) diagrams are network planning diagrams which can be used to show the sequence of activities (or tasks) in a project and the relationship between them. Software programs are again available to help you draw up PERT diagrams and you will find several variations of the technique.

The basic steps you go through are as follows:

I   Start by arranging the different tasks in a logical order. The arrows show which tasks must be completed before the tasks they lead to can start.

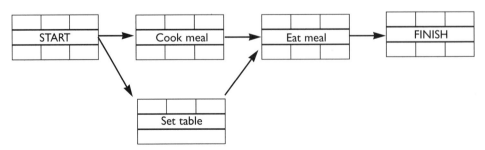

2 Each box in your network needs to contain this information.

Early start		Early finish
	Task name	
Late start		Late finish

3 Fill in the boxes like this:

a Starting at the left of the diagram, fill in the earliest time an activity can start, then its duration. In the example, this is in minutes. Then use the duration to fill in the earliest time the activity can finish. The start and finish times have no duration.

b Move on to the next box and do the same. The earliest start time is always the same as the earliest finish time in the preceding box. If two boxes lead into one, take the later time.

c Then start at the right hand side of the diagram. In the FINISH box, the latest finish time is the same as earliest finish time. Work backwards, using the durations to fill in the latest finish time and the latest start time in each box. The latest finish time is the same as the latest start time in the box connected by an arrow on the right. If you have two latest start times, take the earlier time.

d Finally, fill in the slack time by subtracting the early finish time from the late finish time in each box. If these figures are the same, there is no slack.

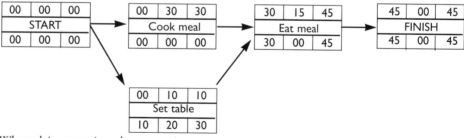

What this exercise shows us is:

■ There is a connected path of activities through the process in which there is no slack. This is the critical path. If any of these activities are delayed, the whole project will be delayed. (The critical path here involves cooking and eating the meal.)

■ Where slack exists, you have some freedom in when you schedule an activity. (You can choose when you set the table.)

■ Nobody needs a PERT diagram to tell them when to set the table. This is not a completely frivolous point. When you have access to tools as a project manager, it is extremely tempting to use them, even when they are not appropriate.

Would PERT diagrams help you plan your project? Why?

PERT diagrams are useful when you are organizing a complex sequence of activities which are dependent upon each other and where you can estimate durations with reasonable certainty. However, they are time-consuming to prepare and not particularly accessible to other people.

GANTT CHARTS

Most people are much more familiar with Gantt charts than with PERT diagrams.

	Weeks						
	1	2	3	4	5	6	7
Activity 1	▨	▨					
Activity 2		▨	▨				
Activity 3			▨	▨			
Activity 4					▨	▨	▨

Gantt charts have a horizontal timescale, which may be measured in hours, days, weeks or months, depending on the scale of your project. The separate activities are listed down the left-hand side. Horizontal bars show when each activity will be taking place.

Gantt charts are a good way of giving an immediate visual impression of what will be happening. Many versions are available commercially, with click-on or adhesive strips. They are also available as software.

The main disadvantages of Gantt charts are that they:

- do not draw attention to dependencies
- can be time-consuming to update

Would Gantt charts help you plan your project? Why?

If your project is relatively small, then Gantt charts probably will be helpful. They are less useful on large, complicated projects and in situations where plans change frequently.

Setting the baseline

Before the implementation stage begins, you will have assembled a detailed project plan. This will cover cost, time, quality and automating the process.

COST

Your project budget is compiled from the estimates you made on the cost of resources. It has several functions:

- It tells the client organization how much money the project will cost
- It tells you how much money you will need, and when you will need it
- It provides a baseline against which you can monitor spending as the project progresses

TIME

You will have prepared a schedule. This may take the form of a network diagram, such as a PERT diagram or a Gantt chart. It is also useful to summarize the schedule so that the key dates, or milestones, can be easily identified. This gives everyone involved an idea of the overall shape of the project.

QUALITY

You will have a work breakdown structure, in which you will record the details of every task to be done. The resources to be used will be linked to your budget and the timing of the tasks will be linked to your schedule.

You will also need other documents to help you monitor quality during the implementation stage. These may include:

- a clear specification of the project's deliverables
- definitions of working methods and procedures
- details of how work will be supervised and reviewed

AUTOMATING THE PROCESS

If your project is small- or medium-sized, it is quite possible to prepare a project plan yourself, with no special equipment. This is how project managers worked for many years. However, sophisticated software packages are now available. These have several advantages. They allow you to:

- store large amounts of information
- update your plans quickly
- explore 'what if' scenarios
- produce reports quickly
- produce professional looking presentations for your clients

However, project management software does have its disadvantages. These programs are usually extremely complex. They may take you a long time to master and can produce results which are too elaborate for your needs, or the needs of the people you are trying to communicate with. There is also a danger that you will become so involved in the model of the project represented on your software that you will become less aware of the realities of the situation.

ACTIVITY 50

Use what you have learned in this section to put together a plan for a project of your own.

FEEDBACK

You should now have a very good idea of how you would like your project to run. In the next section we will look at what happens when you put your plan into action.

Summary

Now that you have finished this section, you should be able to:

- pick an effective team
- manage a team at different stages of its development
- use estimating techniques to plan your use of resources
- specify and obtain the resources you need
- prioritize your resource needs
- produce a work breakdown structure for your project
- use basic flowcharts to plan your project
- use basic PERT diagrams to plan your project
- use Gantt charts to plan your project
- recognize which planning tools are appropriate to your needs

Notes

1 Belbin, M. (1981) *Management Teams: Why They Succeed or Fail* Butterworth-Heinemann.

2 Adapted from Thomson, R. and Mabey, C. (1994) *Developing Human Resources,* Institute of Management Foundation/Butterworth-Heinemann.

3 Baguley, P. *Managing Successful Projects.*

4 Brown, M. *Successful Project Management.*

Section 4
Monitoring, controlling and evaluating

Now we come to the crunch. You have planned your project down to the last detail – and the time has come to put your plans into action. In this final section we will look at the aspects of a project that you need to control, and the techniques you can use to do it.

Every project, you will remember, is unique. This means that, however thorough your planning has been, you are likely to come up against some problems which you had not anticipated. We will look at some things you can do to pull your project back on track.

Every project is a learning experience, especially at the implementation phase. This is when you will find out how effective you really are as a project manager. We end this section with a discussion of how you can evaluate a project and build on your experience.

What do you need to watch?

The people who commissioned your project are primarily interested in three things:

- what you are going to deliver
- when you are going to deliver it
- how much it is going to cost

Your project plans focused on these three elements of quality, time and cost and these are, not surprisingly, also the aspects which you must concentrate on during the implementation phase.

TIME

Imagine that you are taking a train journey. Half an hour out of London, the engine breaks down and it is an hour before a replacement arrives. At this point, you know that you are going to be at least one hour late arriving at your destination. However, because of the delay, you miss your connection at Preston and have to wait another two hours for the next local train. You finally arrive at your destination three hours late.

The same thing happens with projects. Any task which takes longer than you planned may have a direct effect on your final delivery date. It may also have much more serious knock-on effects on other tasks which cannot start until it has been finished. When you monitor time, therefore, you need to be aware of:

- whether you are deviating from your schedule
- the effect of any deviance on dependent parts of the project.

COST

Any deviation from your planned timescale can also affect costs:

The project was designed to last six months. I had leased premises for that period. However, we hit a major problem and things took longer than expected. At the end of the six-month period, I knew we needed another eight weeks before we could deliver. The client understood what was happening and agreed to move the dates. But I had to pay the project team for the extra weeks of the project and also take out another six months lease on the premises, which was a devasting blow to my budget.

You will be aware of major construction projects, such as the building of the Channel Tunnel and the new British Library whose costs have spiralled as the time they have been taken has been extended. The longer a project goes on, the more resources it will need.

Costs can also be affected by:

- changes in the cost of borrowing money
- changes in the prices of materials and equipment
- unexpected events which you did not budget for

It is therefore essential to keep track of whether your actual spending conforms to your forecast budget.

QUALITY

Quality is more difficult to measure, and consequently to monitor, than time and cost. Essentially, what you need to know is how closely your final outcomes will conform to the outcomes your client is expecting. Quality management is based on the principle that you do not wait until a process is finished to see whether the outcome is a success. This is even more important in project management than in the management of on-going operations, because you only have one shot at achieving your outcomes.

As your project is proceeding, you need to monitor that the right things are being done in the right way. You also need to review intermediate outcomes at pre-determined points. These points may concide with the important dates, or milestones, which you set for the project.

ACTIVITY 51

1   Think about a project you have been involved with in the past. Did anything go wrong? If so, did it involve:

   ❑ time?
   ❑ cost?
   ❑ quality?
   ❑ a combination of these things?

2   How quickly was the problem picked up by the project manager?

FEEDBACK

An effective project manager is aware immediately of any significant deviation from the project plan.

HOW MUCH CONTROL DO YOU NEED?

You need to know how closely the project is following your plans, but you also need to keep your eye on the big picture. This is actually the most important part of the project manager's role during the implementation stage. You are probably the only person who will be able to judge the significance of any delay or extra expense. And you can only do this if you keep the final objectives in mind all the time.

The individuals in your team must know exactly what they are supposed to be doing at any time. If you picked people with the right skills and have briefed them properly, you must allow them to get on with things. A mistake that some project managers make is to keep too tight a control on the day-to-day activity of the project team.

I was asked to build a kitchen in an architect designed house. The project manager kept coming in to see how I was doing. Had I remembered to order the fittings? What shade of woodstain was I going to use? Had I forgotten I had to be finished next Wednesday for the plumber to come in? It drove me mad. I'm an experienced carpenter, but he clearly didn't trust me to do the job properly.

You must allow your team a certain amount of autonomy in their work. The more you trust them, in fact, the greater the level of commitment and responsibility they are likely to show. If people feel that they are not trusted, they will be less ready to find creative solutions to problems, or to confide in you if anything does go wrong.

The business of controlling a project can be very time-consuming. Make sure that you are not wasting time monitoring and controlling insignificant details. Concentrate on the aspects of the project which really matter. Also, take care that the administration of the project does not distract your team from their real tasks:

I was trying to edit a series of books. That was my role on the project. But every week I was bombarded with forms from the project manager. I had to account for every hour of my time and constantly assess my progress against the schedule on a daily basis. It got to be ridiculous. In the end, I told the project manager that either she could have the books, or she could have the forms.

ACTIVITY 52

Think about a time at work when you asked somebody to do something for you and it turned out badly.

Did this happen because:

❑ you had not briefed the person properly?
❑ you had picked the wrong person for the job?
❑ you had misunderstood the nature of the task?
❑ something else _____

FEEDBACK

If you ticked any of the first three boxes, the problem could have been avoided before the task began.

How do you know what's going on?

The main way in which a project manager monitors things is by using progress reports. These will be prepared, in the first instance, by the people who are actually doing the work. The project manager, or perhaps other individuals who are responsible for particular parts of the project, will then summarize these reports.

Progress reports should measure how the project is conforming to your plans concerning time and quality. Important information to ask for includes:

- scheduled start and finish times
- when a task actually started
- when it will be finished
- any problems encountered
- the impact any problems may have on other parts of the process

ACTIVITY 53

Design a progress report form you could use on your own project.

FEEDBACK

Are all the questions you included relevant to your project? How easily and quickly could the form be filled in? How easy would it be to compile and evaluate the information it contains?

CONTROLLING COSTS

You need to know what money has been spent (or commited) at any point in the project and how this compares with your estimates. These are the most important statistics you will need:[1]

Estimated at Completion (EAC)

What the total cost of the project will be, as calculated by looking at the plan as it stands, i.e. costs incurred to date + scheduled costs

Budgeted at Completion (BAC)

The total cost derived from the plan before any work began

Actual Cost of Work Performed (ACW)

The amount of money spent so far

Budgeted Cost of Work Performed (BCWP)

What you should have spent to get this far, i.e. the total budgeted cost for the project multiplied by the percentage achieved

Budgeted Cost of Work Scheduled (BCWS)

What you should have spent by this point in time, i.e. the total budgeted cost for the project multiplied by the percentage of elapsed time

---

ACTIVITY 54

What could be happening to your project if:

1 ACWP is more than BCWP?

2 BCWP is more than BCWS?

3 ACWP is less than BCWS?

FEEDBACK

1   This means that it is costing you more than you expected to get the work done.

2   This means that you are ahead of schedule.

3   This could mean that you are behind schedule. Or it could mean that the costs of getting the work done are lower than you expected. You would have to check the ACWP against the BCWP.

In order to have accurate statistics to work with, you must know what money is being spent on behalf of the project. If any individuals apart from yourself have the authority to arrange for payments to be made, they should:

- raise purchase orders first, so that you are aware of these payments in advance
- send the invoices they receive to be checked against the purchase orders and paid centrally

In a large project, you may want to devolve parts of the budget to members of your team. In this situation, they should report back regularly on their progress against budget and alert you to any problems quickly.

KEEPING IN TOUCH

As well as receiving progress reports and checking on the budget, you will also need to keep in personal touch with what is happening. This will involve holding regular team meetings, at which everyone can get a sense of how things are going. It is also important to have one-to-one meetings with members of your team at which you can discuss:

- things which are irrelevant to the rest of the team
- things which you don't want the rest of the team to know about

If you have to talk to an individual about the quality of their work, or to criticize them in any other way, do it in private. Public 'dressings down' will humiliate the person involved and cause divisions amongst the team. You may also be concerned about a particular aspect of the project and want to sort out the implications of what is happening with a team member who has specialist knowledge before you decide what to do.

You should also 'walk the job', going to talk to people informally when they are working. This will give you a feel of what is actually happening and may help you to spot problems before they get out of hand. It is, of course, important not to give people the impression that you are simply coming round to check up on them.

Staying in control

Inevitably, at some point in a project, you will have to update your plans. You will probably have to do it many times. When a change happens, you must consider the impact on other parts of the project. Some of these implications will be obvious to you immediately, but you should also gather information from anyone else who might be affected. One way to do this is to circulate an impact analysis form. This describes the problem and the action you propose to take. It asks for information on:

- tasks affected
- changes to the effort involved in these tasks
- changes to the timing of these tasks
- other dependent tasks which will be affected
- the impact on resources and costs
- the impact on quality
- any other comments

Once you have this information, you can make the necessary adjustments to your plans.

RESOLVING PROBLEMS

When something goes wrong, you have three basic options:

- use your contingency allowance
- find a creative solution to the problem
- changing the parameters on time, cost or quality

Contingency

This is the easiest way to get out of a difficult situation, but it may not be the best solution. You should not use the extra time you have built into your schedules and budgets lightly. There may be other problems further down the line when this is the only solution that is available.

Creative solutions

These are the kind of solutions in which you find another way to achieve your objectives. They usually come when you are able to look at your problem from a different perspective. It may help to:

- talk the problem over with someone who is not involved in the project
- brainstorm the problem

- sleep on it
- re-examine the assumptions you made at the start of the project

ACTIVITY 55

1   In what circumstances do you get your most creative ideas?

2   Could you use this technique in the context of project management? How?

FEEDBACK

Compare your answer with these:

When I have got a problem that I can't solve, I go and dig the garden. By putting maximum effort into something else, I find that when I come back to the problem, it looks slightly different, and I can see a way through.

If something is bothering me, I can't let it go. I use decision trees, mind maps, any tool which will help me look at the problem. I sit and worry at it until I've sorted it out.

Unfortunately, creative solutions cannot be had to order. If you can't come up with one, you may have to alter the parameters of your project.

Time, cost and quality

You may have to change your completion dates. This is not a good solution and can only be done with the agreement of your project sponsor.

You may be able to solve the problem by using more resources. For example, if it is taking a DTP operator longer than expected to complete a report, put somebody else on the job as well. Be aware, however, that anyone who gets involved in a project at a late stage will probably not work as quickly as someone who has been involved for longer, and may also need training. It may also be possible to move staff from a less urgent part of the project without incurring further costs. In doing this, you may be storing up more problems for the future, if they get behind with their own tasks.

You can also change the quality of your outcomes. This could involve delivering:

- less than you promised
- a product that meets your client's needs less exactly.

If the final outcomes of the project are affected, you can only make decisions about whether to sacrifice time, cost or quality in consultation with your client.

WHERE TO DRAW THE LINE

One of the most difficult things to do as a project manager is to know when to insist on your authority, and when you can be flexible. Think about the situation in the following activity.

ACTIVITY 56

You have stressed the importance to your project team of achieving a particular deadline. Late one night, you get a phone call at home from a desperate team member who is trying to complete some graphs for the report you have asked for tomorrow. His computer has just crashed. He can't finish the work unless he drives ten miles and borrows a colleague's machine. He will be up all night. You know that you have built some slack into your schedule and it doesn't really matter if you don't get the report for a couple of days.

What should you say to the team member?

FEEDBACK

If you insist that the team member does the work tonight, you will be putting undue strain on him, which may affect his performance in the next day or so. And if he ever finds out that the report was sitting on your desk for two days after he stayed up all night to complete it, he will be justifiably annoyed.

However, if you tell him that the deadline was not as important as you said it was, you may shake his belief in future deadlines.

In situations like this, you have to balance many factors:

■ your authority as project manager

■ whether you trust the individual concerned

■ how open you are prepared to be with your team

■ your relationship with the project team over the course of the project

■ the needs of the project

■ the needs of the project team

Ideally, you should work towards achieving a situation where your team is committed to the project as you are yourself and can be trusted not to abuse any flexibility you are prepared to give them.

How did it go?

At the end of a project, there are lessons to be learned. If you are working for a large organization, they may instigate their own post-project appraisal. This is usually done by an objective third party and may not happen until some time after the completion of the project, when its long-term effects can be properly assessed. Post-project appraisal will probably involve an examination of project documents and interviews with project staff. A report will be produced, with recommendations which can lead to improvements in later projects in:

■ cost estimation and risk evaluation

■ evaluation of contractors

■ project management techniques

Alternatively, you may be asked by the project sponsor to prepare your own report. This could include:

■ a comparison of what was achieved against the original Terms of Reference

- a report on any problems you encountered in the course of the project, including wrong assumptions that were made at the outset
- any further work, the need for which was revealed by the project but was not included in the final outcomes.

Finally, you should try to learn as much as you can yourself from the project.

ACTIVITY 57   G3.2, G6.2

You can use the following checklist to review and evaluate a project.

1 Were the project objectives fully met?

2 If not, what objectives were missed and why did this happen?

3 Where there any changes to the time, cost and specifications of the project as described in the Terms of Reference?

4 If so, why did this happen?

5 Were all the assumptions made at the start of the project correct?

6 How satisfied was the client with the outcomes of the project?

7 How well did you communicate with your project sponsor?

8 How could you improve communication in the future?

9 What aspects of the project do you think could have gone better?

10 What mistakes were made?

11 How could you avoid them happening again?

12 How well did the members of the project team perform?

13 Could you extend the role of any members of the project team in the future?

14 What were the strengths and weaknesses of your suppliers?

15 How well did you estimate your use of resources?

16 How well did you estimate the time taken to complete tasks?

17 What planning tools did you use, and how effective were they?

18 What documents did you use to monitor and control the project?

19 Would you amend them in any way?

20 What data from the project relating to costs or timing will help you plan a subsequent project more effectively?

21 What knowledge and work-based skills do you need to develop to manage the next project more effectively?

22 What interpersonal skills do you need to develop to manage the next project more effectively?

23 What would you do differently if you were starting the project again now?

Summary

Now that you have finished this section, you should be able to:

- identify the key aspects of a project which you need to monitor and control
- assess the level of control you need to exercise
- use progress reports to control a project
- monitor and control spending in a project
- choose and implement an appropriate method to solve problems
- review and evaluate a project

Notes

1 Brown, M. *Successful Project Management in a Week*, Headway, Hodder & Stoughton/The Institute of Management Foundation, 1992.

Summary

Now that you have finished this book, you should be able to:

- describe the important features of project management
- describe and carry out the role of a project manager at different stages of a project
- identify external and internal forces which work for and against a project
- manage resistance to change associated with a project
- recognize ethical issues relevant to a project
- take account of financial constraints and legal issues which affect project management decisions
- select and manage an effective team
- plan, prioritize, specify and obtain resources to plan a project
- select and use appropriate techniques to plan a project
- monitor and control the key aspects of a project
- select and use an appropriate method to solve problems
- review and evaluate a project

Recommended reading

Baguley, P. (1995). *Managing Successful Projects: A Guide For Every Manager*, Pitman Publishing/The Institute of Management Foundation

Broadbent, M. and Cullen, J. (1993). *Managing Financial Resources,* Butterworth-Heinemann/The Institute of Management Foundation

Brown, M. (1992). *Successful Project Management in a Week*, Headway, Hodder & Stoughton/The Institute of Management Foundation

Hardy, G. (1996). *Successfully Managing Change in a Week*, Headway, Hodder & Stoughton/The Institute of Management Foundation

Jay, R. (1995). *Build a Great Team!*, Pitman Publishing/The Institute of Management Foundation

Moran, K. (1995) *Investment Appraisal for Non-Financial Managers: A Step-by-Step Guide To Making Profitable Decisions*, Pitman Publishing and the Institute of Management Foundation

Norton, B. and D'Vaz, G. (1995). *Project Management*, Management Directions/The Institute of Management Foundation

Checklist 005: Performing a SWOT analysis and *Checklist 035: Managing Projects*, The Institute of Management Foundation

About the Institute of Management

The mission of the Institute of Management (IM) is to promote the development, exercise and recognition of professional management.

The IM is the leading professional organization for managers. Its efforts and resources are devoted to ensuring the continuing development and success of its members.

At the forefront of management standards, the IM provides a range of services for its members. These include flexible training programmes and a unique range of support services such as career counselling, enquiry and research facilities and preferential prices on IM publications and other IM products.

Further details about the Institute of Management may be obtained from:

Institute of Management
Management House
Cottingham Road
Corby
Northants
NN17 1TT

Telephone 01536 204222

We need your views

We really need your views in order to make the Institue of Management Open Learning Programme an even better learning tool for you. Please take time out to complete and return this questionnaire to Tessa Gingell, Pergamon Open Learning, Linacre House, Jordan Hill, Oxford OX2 8DP.

Name:...

Address:..

....

Title of workbook:...

If applicable, please state which qualification you are studying for. If not, please describe what study you are undertaking, and with which organization or college:

....

Please grade the following out of 10 (10 being extremely good, 0 being extremely poor):

Content: ....   Suitability for ability level: ....

Readability: ....   Qualification coverage: ....

What did you particularly like about this workbook?

....

Are there any features you disliked about this workbook? Please identify them.

....

Are there any errors we have missed?
If so, please state page number: ....

How are you using the material? For example, as an open learning course, as a reference resource, as a training resource, etc.

....

How did you hear about the Institue of Management Open Learning Programme?:

Word of mouth: Through my tutor/trainer: Mailshot:

Other (please give details):..

Many thanks for your help in returning this form.

Institute of Management Open Learning Programme

This programme comprises seventeen workbooks, each on a core management topic with the latest management thinking, as well as a *User Guide* and a *Mentor Guide*.

Designed for self study through open learning, the workbooks cover all management experience from team building to budgeting, from the skills of self management to manage strategically for organizational success.

TITLE	ISBN	Price
The Influential Manager	0 7506 3662 9	£22.50
Managing Yourself	0 7506 3661 0	£22.50
Getting the Right People to Do the Right Job	0 7506 3660 2	£22.50
Understanding Business Process Management	0 7506 3659 9	£22.50
Customer Focus	0 7506 3663 7	£22.50
Getting TQM to Work	0 7506 3664 5	£22.50
Leading from the Front	0 7506 3665 3	£22.50
Improving Your Organization's Success	0 7506 3666 1	£22.50
Project Management	0 7506 3667 X	£22.50
Budgeting and Financial Control	0 7506 3668 8	£22.50
Effective Financial and Resource Management	0 7506 3669 6	£22.50
Developing Yourself and Your Staff	0 7506 3670 X	£22.50
Building a High Performance Team	0 7506 3671 8	£22.50
The New Model Leader	0 7506 3672 6	£22.50
Making Rational Decisions	0 7506 3673 4	£22.50
Communication	0 7506 3674 2	£22.50
Successful Information Management	0 7506 3675 0	£22.50
User Guide	0 7506 3676 9	£22.50
Mentor Guide	0 7506 3677 7	£22.50
Full set of workbooks plus *Mentor Guide* and *User Guide*	0 7506 3359 X	£370.00

To order: *(Please quote ISBNs when ordering)*

- College Orders: 01865 314333
- Account holders: 01865 314301
- Individual Purchases: 01865 314627

(Please have credit card details ready)

For further information or to request a full series brochure, please contact:

Tessa Gingell on 01865 314477